ROBERT HALF'S
SUCCESS GUIDE
FOR ACCOUNTANTS

ROBERT HALF'S SUCCESS GUIDE FOR ACCOUNTANTS

Robert Half

McGraw-Hill Book Company

New York   St. Louis   San Francisco   Auckland
Bogotá   Hamburg   Johannesburg   London   Madrid
Mexico   Montreal   New Delhi   Panama   Paris
São Paulo   Singapore   Sydney   Tokyo   Toronto

Library of Congress Cataloging in Publication Data

Half, Robert.
    Robert Half's Success guide for accountants.

    Includes index.
    1. Accounting—Vocational guidance.   I. Title.
II. Title Success guide for accountants.
HF5657.H34   1984   657'.023'73   83-18688
ISBN 0-07-025569-5

1234567890 DOC/DOC 89876543

ISBN 0-07-025569-5

The editors for this book were Bonnie Binkert and Esther Gelatt, the designer was Dennis Sharkey, and the production supervisor was Teresa F. Leaden. It was set in Baskerville by Achorn Graphics, Inc. Printed and bound by R. R. Donnelley & Sons Company.

CONTENTS

PREFACE

Success has to start somewhere.
Failure needs no beginning.

As an accountant, you do not need to be told that the accounting profession has been changing dramatically over the past two decades and that these changes have opened up extraordinary career opportunities. It's true, of course, that accounting has always been a basic tool in business, but a number of factors—increased government requirements, frequently changing tax legislation, the information revolution, to name just three—have greatly enhanced the role that accountants now play in business. It's hardly a coincidence that today more chief executive officers than ever before are coming out of accounting or financial backgrounds.

If the profession has been changing dramatically, so, too, have the criteria for career success in accounting. The biggest change is simply this: if you aspire to the upper levels of public or management accounting, you can no longer build your career path around technical competence alone. It's not enough, in other words, to be a good "numbers" person. Just as important (if not more important) are skills that have less to do with accounting per se and more to do with your general business acumen and your effectiveness as a person.

Which brings me to this book.

Its purpose is not to make you a "better accountant" in the strict sense of the phrase. Its purpose instead is to show you how you can take the accounting skills you already have and parlay these skills into greater career success.

The advice you'll be receiving in this book is based, in part, on the more than 35 years that I myself have been involved in the career aspects of accounting. But to assure the relevance and the value of the material, I took two additional steps. First, I commissioned Burke Marketing Research to conduct a survey exclusively for this book. The purpose of the survey was to gain insight into the career aspects of accounting from the people in the best position to offer this insight: from managing partners, top management, and personnel directors. Second, I interviewed personally some two dozen of the most successful accountants and executives in North America and I incorporated their observations on career success in accounting into each of the chapters in this book.

The findings that turned up in our survey and in the observations that came out of the interviews should be of interest to every accountant who aspires to a greater degree of career success. They constitute, all in all, important, timely, and highly practical advice on how to manage the most important aspect of your accounting career: yourself.

Robert Half

ACKNOWLEDGMENTS

No one has ever achieved anything without help.

In a sense, nearly every accountant I have worked with over the past 35 years has contributed in one way or another to this book, but there are certain people to whom I owe a special debt of gratitude. Many of these people are highly successful accountants and business people who, busy as they are, allowed me to interview them and in their answers to my questions provided much of the insightful advice that appears throughout the book. Their names, as well as the names of others who were instrumental in this project, are: William Aiken, Bob L. Anderson, Kenneth S. Asch, Nancy P. Asch, Isaac Assael, Norman E. Auerbach, Colin Ayley, Abraham Bailis, Frank Bartl, Bonnie Binkert, Richard M. Bird, Dr. Abraham J. Briloff, Dr. James Bulloch, Michael Burgio, Philip B. Chenok, Alex Cohen, Frank M. Davidson, Roger E. Davidson, Bryce Dunahoo, Malcolm S. Forbes, A. Bernard Frechtman, Patricia Frechtman, Lester K. Fromin, Marshall Fudge, Alvin M. Galland, Charles R. Gallegly, Gerald G. Gilberg, Larry Gipple, Harry A. Gilbert, Michael Goldstein, Viola Gouty, A. S. Grishman, Maxine E. Half, Valeries Hannah, Thomas Hannah, Merton Hersh, Richard S. Hickok, Neil R. Hurst, Thomas Hurst, William S. Kanaga, William E. Kinol, Richard K. Kleinert, Eugene Koshner, Siegbert Levisohn, Steven E.

Lieberman, Percy M. Lincoln, Jr., Edward O. Lutz, Mary McCary, Buddy Martin, Kenneth Majcen, Eli Mason, Vernon L. Mathiesen, Robert Maynard, Robert McCall, Morton M. Meisels, Larry Miller, William J. Morgan, Bruce Morris, Thomas Murphy, Herbert J. Myers, Howard Narlinger, Caryn Newman, David Newman, John Noble, Denis J. O'Leary, Dennis A. Osterdock, Robert A. Palmer, Charles Peterson, Donald F. Prince, Daniel K. Roberts, R. B. Rowley, Edward J. Rozhon, Jeffrey Rozhon, Stephen L. Ryter, Dr. Emanuel Saxe, Barbara J. Shildneck, Robert Shultis, Marc J. Silbert, Peggy L. Silbert, Saul S. Silverman, Peter Skomorowsky, Ronald R. Smith, Edwin W. Southerland, Patrick L. Southerland, Charles L. Squires, Gordon R. Starnes, Barry Tarshis, Sanford Teller, Graham Thompson, Michael Uhls, Thomas Uhls, William F. Wernersback, Charles J. Wolff, and John Woodcock.

ROBERT HALF'S
SUCCESS GUIDE
FOR ACCOUNTANTS

CHAPTER ONE **ACCOUNTING: A GOOD PLACE TO BE**

Accounting for your future is your most important accounting function.

A young man I know recently took a job in the sales division of a well-known electronics company. There would be nothing unusual about someone taking such a job, except that this particular young man is a trained accountant who, in fact, had been working for the past four years in the company's internal auditing department.

Why the change? "I didn't think I was getting anywhere," he explained to me, and then went on to point out that he wasn't happy with the salary he was earning as an auditor, that he wasn't deriving any feeling of accomplishment from his position, and that he didn't feel as if he was getting enough respect for the work he was doing. He also complained that in his company accountants were considered "overhead," and that the "real producers" were in sales. "I was getting more and

1

more frustrated," he said. "I had the feeling that nobody in the company recognized what I was doing. So when a job opened up in sales, I asked for it and got it."

As it happens, the accountant I've just described is not a rarity. Accounting, like other professions, is not without its share of professionals who are frustrated and discontented. Numerous surveys published over the past several years indicate that accountants as a group are dissatisfied with *many* elements of their jobs—in particular, their salaries, their lack of recognition, and their working conditions. And some surveys show that the areas in which accountants express either a "lack of satisfaction" or "complete dissatisfaction" actually outnumber the areas in which they say they are satisfied.

So you can't really blame somebody like the young man I'm talking about here for giving up on accounting as a career. It may well be that many of you reading this book have either contemplated or are now contemplating a similar move, even though you may be an excellent accountant with many years of experience. Chances are, too, that it isn't the work itself that you're unhappy with (most accountants, according to surveys taken on the subject, enjoy the actual work), but the situation in your firm, your department, or your practice.

You may feel, for instance, that you're not making the money you should be making for the work you do and the contributions you make to the clients you serve. You may know business people or lawyers who are further along in their careers than you, even though you feel you are more intelligent and have a better knowledge of business in general. You may be working for a CPA firm that, in your view, isn't giving you the opportunity to make meaningful decisions. You may be a management accountant in a large company that, as you see it, doesn't attach enough value to your work or, for that matter, the work of your entire department. And maybe you're beginning to think you made a mistake by becoming an accountant in the first place. Perhaps you've come to the conclusion that, as one disgruntled accountant I know once said, "The only way to get ahead in accounting is to get out of it."

As somebody whose specialty for 35 years has been filling accounting and other financial positions, I understand and sympathize with these sentiments. I would be the last person to suggest that the complaints accountants are voicing today are unjustified. In my view, many accountants do *not* command either the salaries or the respect they deserve, considering the services they provide. Unfortunately, many corporations today do see accountants as overhead rather than producers.

In spite of these conditions, in spite of the gap between what accountants do and what some accountants receive in the way of money and recognition, the last thing I would ever recommend to an accountant today is to abandon accounting. I'll go even further. If anything, accounting may well be today's *best* route to a successful business career; if I myself were a young man starting in college today, accounting would again be my major field of study.

I base this bullish outlook on a number of factors. First of all, unlike many other professions today (medicine and teaching, for example), the demand for accountants appears to be growing, not shrinking, though the growth rate is not as pronounced as it was in the late 1960s and early 1970s. In 1981, *Forbes* magazine, while noting that graduates with accounting degrees will rise from 59,000 in 1981 to 70,000 in 1985, maintained nonetheless that "demand will outstrip supply," and a 1982 survey by the American Institute of Certified Public Accountants (AICPA) indicated a 7 percent growth rate in demand for public accountants throughout the rest of the decade.

These encouraging statistics, moreover, are backed up by the findings of a survey conducted by Burke Marketing Research expressly for this book. I'll be referring to the various findings of this important survey throughout the book, but the particular finding of interest here is that nearly 90 percent of the chief financial officers, CPA partners, top management personnel, and personnel directors queried felt that opportunities in today's business climate were "better than ever" for accountants. The results of our survey were reinforced by the views of virtually all the accountants and business executives I interviewed for this book. As Malcolm S. Forbes, chairman of *Forbes* magazine, told me, "Things are going to be more complicated in business, not less, and this means that accountants are going to be in more demand."

Other reasons—reasons that go beyond statistics—support the view that accounting is an excellent field to be in these days. The recession in the early 1980s, for one thing, has produced a dramatic shift in corporate priorities, with the result that major corporations are far more concerned today than ever before with financial planning and are relying more and more on their own financial personnel and on their public accounting firms to help them make key decisions. At the same time, the ever increasing reporting and auditing requirements being placed on U.S. businesses by the IRS, the SEC, the FTC, and the rest of the government alphabet, have given added stature and power to business accounting departments. In many companies the number of internal accountants has more than doubled over the past three or four years.

Finally, we're seeing more and more corporations choosing as their chief executive officers managers with accounting and financial backgrounds. According to a *Fortune* magazine survey, nearly 25 percent of the 800 highest paid CEOs in the United States have financial backgrounds. Among them are CPAs such as Paul F. Oreffice of Dow Chemical, Thomas A. Murphy of General Motors, and James L. Kettelson of Tenneco.

So the opportunities in accounting are there—and they are growing. They are particularly good for women. Accounting may well offer women the best overall route for moving ahead quickly. Granted, on partnership levels women are still a rarity in public accounting, but as more and more women enter the profession, it's only a matter of time until the proportion of women partners grows. The publication *Boardroom Reports* went so far recently as to assert that in 10 years "more than half of the new-partner admissions" in the largest public accounting firms would be women.[1] This is *Boardroom Reports'* rationale, based on the views of a current partner with a major CPA firm: "It is generally accepted that the best business students today are women."

Meanwhile, the most recent surveys show that some 40 percent of college graduates with accounting degrees are women and that women represent nearly a third of the young recruits in the larger firms. In addition, a survey my company recently did showed that when a man and a woman competed for the same accounting job (the jobs paid between $15,000 and $50,000), the woman got the job 72 percent of the time. "The good news for women in accounting," says a woman editor in the accounting field, "is that they're no longer perceived as full-charge bookkeepers but as accountants. Women are more visible than ever before in the profession, and the top firms are going out of their way to hire them."

HOW THE PROFESSION IS CHANGING

At the root of these broadened opportunities in accounting are a number of dramatic changes that have occurred in the profession over the past quarter-century—changes I'm sure you know about. Gone are the days, for instance, when the major public accounting firms confined their activities to pure accounting and based their practices almost entirely on auditing. Today, it is the rare public accounting firm of any size that doesn't have its own tax or management advisory services (MAS) department and isn't relying more and more on the fees from these services. Not long ago Arthur Andersen reported that its fees from

---

[1] I have chosen not to use the term "Big 8" throughout this book in deference to the growing number of practitioners who feel that the term creates the mistaken impression that the number of major public accounting firms is limited to only eight and that big is better.

consulting services were up 30 percent from the previous year and were the prime contributor to a 21 percent increase in overall fees. Interestingly, too, while accounting and auditing represented 61 percent of Andersen's chargeable hours, these two services accounted for only 54 percent of its revenue. Why? The average fee per hour for auditing is less than those for tax and consulting work.

Gone, too, are the days when CPA firms were loathe to advertise their services or compete directly with one another for major accounts. What's happened in accounting is similar to what has happened, to a great extent, in the investment industry, in banking, and in law. The traditional, leisurely—formerly called "gentlemanly"—way of doing business has given way to a more aggressive, more openly competitive business style. Typifying this new style has been an increase in allegations that the larger public accounting firms are "low balling" (underbidding) in order to get a new client—a practice that was unheard of as recently as 10 years ago.

The changes I've just mentioned were chronicled not long ago by a Chicago *Sun Times* reporter named Mark Brown, who noted, among other things, that Coopers & Lybrand had engaged the firm of New Dimensions Marketing to do its public relations and that Deloitte Haskins & Sells, in the spring of 1979, became the first international public accounting firm to embark on a major advertising campaign. Brown also made note of Alexander Grant's decision in 1982 to hold a press conference on the new federal tax legislation 2 weeks before President Reagan signed the bill. "While the competition was snarling at their audacity," wrote Brown, "Alexander Grant basked in two weeks of press clippings." Brown added: "That kind of clawing might not be unusual in most of the business world, but it is for most accounting firms, many of whom still hang on to their old euphemism for marketing—'practice development' or PD."

Not everyone in accounting is pleased with the direction in which the profession has been moving over the past few years. Some people, for instance, feel that the increasing involvement in MAS presents an inherent conflict of interest for the larger CPA firms, as does the growing involvement of large CPA firms in executive recruiting. How can you maintain your independence, some people want to know, when the client you're auditing is also an MAS client or has key personnel that you yourself have recruited and placed?

Also, not everyone is pleased that the profession has become so competitive that the power in many firms lies not with the most skilled accountants but with accountants who can bring in the most business. The June 1982 issue of *Management Accounting* quoted an Englishman, Anthony Hilton, who saw the increased competition among the big CPA firms as an "undignified scramble—a quite open effort to steal clients," a view shared by more than a few American accountants.

In any case, the trend toward a more competitive, broader-based profession is so well entrenched that in some of the larger firms, MAS services now account for as much as 15 percent of yearly revenues. No one is surprised anymore when, say, Coopers & Lybrand is hired by Sun Oil Company to set up an inventory system for Sun's gasoline products or by American Can to improve cash management. No one is surprised when Arthur Andersen is hired by a large waste disposal system in Chicago to design an information system for its chemical division, or when Price Waterhouse is hired by the U.S. Postal Service to design and put into operation a payroll system capable of processing checks for 700,000 postal workers.

What it all means is that while career prospects for accountants have never been better, there are new demands on accountants who hope to become more successful. It is no longer enough to be a competent technician—not if your ambition is to reach the upper echelons of the profession. With rare exceptions, the accountants who are moving ahead quickly today are men and women whose skills go well beyond the basic tools of the trade. They are good business people, good managers, good communicators, and, in many cases, good salespeople. They are men and women who, in the words of Donald C. Agnew, southwestern managing partner for the CPA firm of Main Hurdman, "are able to translate accounting knowledge into business knowledge and are able to channel their capacity for leadership into productive results." Or, as Malcolm Forbes puts it, "What is really in high demand in accounting is intelligence, the ability to not only produce the numbers but to dig out the meaning of them. An intelligent accountant has an unlimited future."

Virtually all the professionals I interviewed for this book expressed the same basic viewpoint as Malcolm Forbes and Donald Agnew—that is, to get ahead in accounting, you need to be more than an accountant in the traditional sense of the term. William Morgan, a CPA who is a partner in the Short Hills, New Jersey, office of Peat Marwick Mitchell, stresses certain personality traits for accountants who want to get ahead in the profession. "The need today," he says, "is for individuals who are aggressive, inquisitive, and highly motivated." Patrick Lamkin Southerland, a CPA who heads the Robert Half Washington, D.C., franchise, points out that the higher you move up the ladder in accounting, the more important nonaccounting skills become. "Particularly," says Southerland, "the ability to interact with people throughout the company—the ability to not only analyze what is happening but to present that analysis in a politically astute way."

Alvin M. Galland, a CPA who is the chief financial officer of my firm, feels that more than ever before, a management accountant today must be a generalist: "someone who can take financial information and apply it to a variety of issues." And Michael Goldstein, national managing partner of professional services with Laventhol & Horwath, stresses the selling aspect of accounting today. "The accountant in the past," he says, "was able to go off into a corner to work and would still be able to keep clients. No more. The field today is much more competitive, and selling is a major part of what you have to do to succeed."

What all these people are saying, in short, is that the era of the green-eyeshade accountant is now over. If you want to get ahead in accounting today, you can't rely on technical proficiency alone. You need general business and interpersonal skills: your overall business acumen, your ability to manage and motivate, and your ability to assume a direct role in your company's growth.

WHAT THIS BOOK WILL DO FOR YOU

It is not the purpose of this book to make you a "better" accountant per se. I'm assuming that you understand your profession and that you're a solid technician. I am not going to try to increase your knowledge of tax law, make you a better auditor, or improve your financial planning skills. Instead, I will focus on skills that relate purely to *career* success in today's business climate: to the things you should know and to the things you should be doing to *use* the skills and knowledge you've developed in your professional experience and in school to further your career goals, whether these goals lie within the accounting profession or in the corporate world as a whole.

What will concern us is not so much how "good" an accountant you are, but how effectively you are now structuring and managing your career; how you handle yourself on the job; how you deal with the people you work for and work with; how you communicate, delegate, and manage; and how you market and promote yourself—in other words, how you do all the things that, as you will see, are as instrumental to your success as your technical knowledge and skills.

My premise for getting ahead in accounting is a simple one: To generate the highest level of career success from your accounting background and knowledge, your expertise has to extend *beyond* the balance sheet and the profit and loss statement. To reach these levels, you have to think of yourself as a business person *first* and as an accountant second.

Don't misunderstand me. I'm not downplaying the importance of technical skills and knowledge. Nor do I contend that business acumen and managerial expertise are more important than the basic disciplines of this profession. As I indicated earlier, the demand for accountants is growing, but the critical shortage in accounting today isn't so much of technicians as of accountants who can think and perform beyond the normal spheres of accounting. The shortage is of accountants who can manage effectively, communicate effectively, and function as executives and business people rather than as financial specialists.

What are the skills that underlie these functions? How do they relate to accounting? How do you develop them? These are just some of the questions into which we'll look. The answers come from a variety of sources: from surveys and studies, from interviews with people who have parlayed their knowledge of accounting into highly successful careers, and from my own experience as the head of the world's largest recruiting company specializing in accounting and financial personnel.

Above all, I want to prove to you that there is no great mystery to becoming successful in accounting and that people who are at the top of the profession today weren't simply lucky enough to be in the right place at the right time.

I've come to know one accountant very well over the years, a man I'll call Fred. I mention Fred because he is highly successful today—the president of a corporation that manufactures electrical components. Still, not very long ago, Fred considered himself a failure as an accountant. When I first met Fred, about 12 years ago, he'd been through 4 different jobs in less than 6 years, and he was so disenchanted with accounting that he was thinking of getting out of it. "I'm just not a good numbers person," he insisted. "I don't really belong in accounting."

True, Fred *wasn't* a particularly good numbers person. But he had other skills. He got along well with people. He had good managerial skills. And he knew how to plan and coordinate long-term projects. He was much better, in other words, with people than he was with numbers.

Fred had some interesting choices to make. He could have abandoned accounting altogether and moved into some other area—marketing, for instance. But he didn't. Instead, he applied for—and got—an accounting position in which the major part of his job was supervising other accountants. He flourished. Within a year or two, he was promoted to controller, then treasurer, and, ultimately, to the presidency of the firm. Today he is one of the most successful accountants I know.

I grant you, success stories like this one are not everyday occurrences. But the lesson at the root of Fred's story is one that all accountants might well take to heart. Some people might contend that Fred was "lucky" to land a job in a company that suited his particular skills. But I have always believed that the luckiest people are the people who work the hardest at being lucky. I agree, Fred was fortunate to find a job that would eventually lead to a presidency. But it wasn't luck that led him to seek the job he eventually took, and it wasn't luck that he did so well in the job.

What happened to Fred—the success he achieved—can happen to you, and it can happen in any number of different ways: as a partner in a CPA firm, as the controller or president of a company, as a successful practitioner on your own, or in countless business situations in which you're using your accounting background. "The horizons accountants have today are so exciting," says Saul S. Silverman, a successful CPA and attorney, "that anyone with a good level of competitive desire and the desire to serve *must* be successful." Yes, you can go far in accounting, farther than you may think. And I'm going to do my best to point you in the right direction.

CHAPTER TWO DO YOU REALLY WANT TO BE SUCCESSFUL?

The easy way to success is to work hard.

Vic Braden, the well-known tennis coach and television personality, often talks about a conversation he once overheard between a tournament promoter and the tennis champion Jimmy Connors. The tournament director was trying to interest Connors in his tournament, and Connors wanted to know about the prize money.

"Well," said the tournament director. "If you come in first, you win $30,000. And if you come in second. . . ."

He never got a chance to finish the sentence. Said Connors, "I'm not interested in second place."

Indeed he wasn't. And the fact is, if you talk to highly successful people in any field, from tennis to accounting, you're going to find substantially the same attitude: no special interest in second place. I'll go even further. Of all the attributes that characterize highly successful people, in general, and highly successful accountants, in particular, none is more universal than the simple *desire* to succeed. As Richard S. Hickok, CPA, chairman of Main Hurdman, likes to put it, "The one thing

10

nearly all successful accountants have in common is that they are not satisfied with the success they currently enjoy."

Mind you, I'm not suggesting that to be successful in accounting, the only thing you really need is a great *desire* to be successful. Hardly. Accounting, after all, is a complex and demanding field, and if you lack the intelligence, the judgment, the technical skills, and the discipline this complexity requires, you're not going to get very far, regardless of how ambitious you are.

On the other hand, what's lacking in most of the accountants I have met over the past 35 years is not technical skills or intelligence. What's lacking is the ability—and, in many cases, the desire—to direct these technical skills to a predetermined goal. What's lacking is a true commitment to success.

Let me point out quickly that by "commitment to success," I'm not implying a *compulsion* to succeed—a drive so deep that you ignore everything else in your life, in particular your family. On the contrary. As Charles A. Garfield, a California psychologist who has studied hundreds of top performers in business and other fields, points out, optimal performers are not, as a rule, workaholics or the so-called type A behavior personality. They take vacations, they know when to stop working, and they are good at managing their stress.

On the other hand, regardless of your capabilities, you can't take success for granted. You have to *want* it, and you have to go after it. You need what I like to think of as a healthy appetite for success. You need to establish success (however you choose to define it) as an important goal for yourself, and you have to organize a good portion of your life *toward* that goal.

"Nearly all of the successful accountants I know," says Professor Edward O. Lutz, a CPA who is the director of accounting programs at Brooklyn College, "are success-oriented in one way or another. They have their own success goals. In some cases, it may be to become the best technician. In other cases, it might be to become the managing partner of a major CPA firm. Whatever it is, they are *aiming* for something."

It's worth pointing out that Edward Lutz's own success goals underwent a dramatic change in the middle of his career. For 20 years, starting in the late 1940s, he was both an instructor at Brooklyn College and a partner in his own accounting practice. "The only trouble," he says, "is that I was working 80 hours a week and my wife didn't want to be a rich young widow. So, I opted to get out of my accounting business and teach. I wanted to reduce my obligations, live longer, and I decided there was no point in storing up more money. I wanted to enjoy life. Analyzing both of my careers, I decided to give up the headlines and the pressures of public accounting and to continue being just a college professor."

Lutz's career is instructive to think about for a couple of reasons. First of all, it underscores the fact that success doesn't come without hard work. Second, it illustrates the fact that success is a relative concept. Lutz, like many successful accountants, reached a stage in his career in which he felt fulfilled. Had he been a different person, he might have reached this point much earlier, or much later. The point to bear in mind, however, is that Lutz made this decision himself: It wasn't made for him.

I'm not maintaining that the only way to become successful is to work 80 hours a week, and I recognize the crucial difference between being committed to success and being a workaholic—someone who has nothing else in his or her life *except* work. Even so, it's important to recognize that success is not a game you can play now and then when the spirit moves you. You have to play the game on a constant basis; the part of your mind concerned with success should be "on call" at all times.

When you take a vacation, for instance, you shouldn't need to bring work with you. On the other hand, if, on your vacation, you meet someone who might be helpful to your career, you would be foolish not to establish contact and make arrangements to meet when the two of you are back at work.

Here's another example of what I'm talking about. I myself enjoy what I think is an active leisure life. I travel. I play golf. I read. But whatever I'm doing, I always carry a small notebook and pen—or, often, a mini-tape recorder. That way, if an idea occurs to me, I can write it down or record it immediately. In fact, I developed many of the thoughts for this book while walking or driving. I would also suggest that you keep a pad and pen (the kind of pen that has a built-in light), or a recorder, on the night table beside your bed. You never know when you will wake up in the middle of the night with an idea or a solution to a problem you've been trying to solve all day.

These are little things, and you may think of them as inconsequential. However, success is often nothing more than the combined effect of a number of "inconsequentials." Think about it a minute. Think about how much more productive you would be if you could train your mind to function 24 hours a day—not in order to be consumed with work 24 hours a day, but to be receptive at any time to any idea that could be helpful in your career.

SUCCESS PATTERNS IN ACCOUNTING

Over the past several years, there have been a number of studies on the traits that make people successful. I know of no study done specifically on accountants, but I have developed my own ideas on the subject, based on interviews I've had with some of the most successful people in the field. As far as I've been able to tell, most people at the top of the accounting profession share the following traits:

- They view getting ahead as a goal unto itself.
- They work very hard.
- They aren't afraid to put themselves on the line.
- They like what they do and are guided by "internal" goals of excellence.
- They have a great deal of intellectual curiosity.

These are not the *only* traits successful accountants share, but they are the traits that have emerged over and over again in the many conversations I've had with leading accountants. Let's look at each a little more closely.

GETTING AHEAD AS A GOAL UNTO ITSELF

Norman E. Auerbach is a CPA and attorney who for many years was the chairman of Coopers & Lybrand. He began his professional accounting career in 1947 with Lybrand, Ross Bros. & Montgomery (Coopers & Lybrand). William Aiken is a CPA and partner in Main Hurdman and a past president of the National Association of Black Accountants. He began his career as a clerk-typist and then joined the Marines so that he could take advantage of the GI bill and attend college at night.

Here we have two accountants with entirely different career paths, yet sharing one thing in common: a driving desire to move up the success ladder.

Norman Auerbach is interesting not only for what he did while he was *in* accounting but for what he planned to do when he reached the mandatory retirement age of 62. In the early 1950s, while he was moving up the ranks at his firm, Auerbach attended night school at St. John's University to earn a law degree. He was admitted to the bar in 1955, but he never had a chance to practice law until he retired as chairman at Coopers & Lybrand and accepted an offer to associate himself with a law firm. "This is something that as a young man I always wanted to do," he explains. "Only it's happening a 'few years' later."

William Aiken, unlike Auerbach, worked for a number of different organizations after getting into accounting. His first accounting job was as a senior accounting clerk. He then became a state insurance examiner, spent some time with Arthur Young, partnered his own firm for a while, and then went to work in New York City as deputy commissioner of human resources before assuming his present affiliation.

The steady rise of these two men typifies a pattern you will find among most accountants who have achieved a high level of success. But this pattern happens to differ dramatically from the pattern that typifies that of most accountants—finding a comfortable niche and staying there. "One of the main things that often holds accountants back today," says Richard Hickok, "is that some people become satisfied with whatever level they're at and don't feel the need to move upward."

There is nothing *wrong* with being so satisfied with your present job that you're not really interested in bettering your position. If you are happy in your present situation, I don't want to stir up discontent. The question you need to ask yourself, however, is whether your satisfaction is genuine or is a reflection of your lack of confidence—a feeling that you're lucky to be where you are and shouldn't concern yourself with moving forward.

Years ago, I can remember an accountant coming to me and saying he wanted a job but didn't want to be paid more than $80 a week. (As you can see, this was quite a while ago.) When I told him he could probably get a job that paid more, he wasn't interested. "As long as I'm making only $80 a week," he told me, "I know I won't be under that much pressure, and if business gets bad, I won't be laid off."

There is an inherent risk in this attitude. The risk is that as you grow older, your image of yourself could improve and produce a sudden desire to strive for a higher position—but by then, it might be too late to make the move you're thinking about. You'll already have been pigeonholed. Besides, your records will not demonstrate achievement and advancement.

The point is very simple. If you're going to set career goals, you're better off aiming slightly too high than aiming slightly too low.

THE IMPORTANCE OF WORKING HARD

Nobody would argue the fact that accounting is hard work, but as Bob Anderson, my Chicago franchisee, points out, to be highly successful in this field, you really have to go *beyond* the work ethic. "The one thing I've learned about this profession," says Anderson, "is that if you're not willing to work the longest hours, you're going to hold yourself back." By way of example, Anderson cites an early experience in which he was working in the accounting department of a major corporation but wasn't terribly pleased with his situation. "There were six accountants on each side of the room," he says, "and they all had three-piece suits and calculators. It was a stifling environment, and I wanted out."

Anderson eventually got out of this environment, but not without putting in a great deal of extra work. It seems that the assistant treasurer of the company, who was also the manager of two finance companies, had a bookkeeping problem and needed some extra work done. Anderson volunteered. "I did *more* than I had to do, and the net result was that the assistant treasurer eventually created a full-time position for me as his assistant." From there Anderson became an accounting manager for one of the company's subsidiaries and was subsequently promoted to senior consolidation accountant. Eventually, he assumed the controllership of a smaller company.

Bob Anderson's success path convincingly illustrates what psychologist Charles Garfield refers to as "avoiding the comfort zone." Anderson was a good enough accountant, certainly, to have fit in very nicely in that first niche, but he wanted more. More important, he was willing to do the extra work to move out of that zone. His story is not at all unusual among successful people.

BEING WILLING TO PUT YOURSELF ON THE LINE

"An accountant," says Norman Auerbach, "who is reluctant to make a decision for fear of being wrong will not move ahead." Auerbach goes so far as to rate the willingness to make decisions as one of the most important factors in a successful accounting career. "You need confidence in your judgment," says Auerbach, "and a willingness *to be wrong*. Nobody—not even the most successful manager—is right *all* the time."

As it happens, Auerbach worked for a firm where "we gave young people the opportunity to make decisions." He adds that decision making doesn't come naturally to people. "Your judgement will improve," he says, "if you have basic intelligence, and you practice decision making."

The problem with making decisions, of course, is that every decision embodies a certain amount of risk, and because so many decisions in accounting are related directly to the bottom line, the decisions take on more importance. Maybe this is why so many accountants shy away from the decision-making aspect of the profession.

What's lacking in many accountants is a quality that publisher Malcolm Forbes chooses to call "imagination." "With some notable exceptions," Forbes told me, "accountants are too cost conscious and figure conscious to let their imaginations go. Too often, they fail to recognize—or even care about—the *significance* of the numbers." Forbes goes on to cite as one of the major failings of accountants in general, the failure to give "life" to figures, although he recognizes the problems that accountants are usually up against. "Accounting is such a tough discipline," he says, "that the characteristics required to do the basic work correctly often smother the other ingredients of success."

True enough. The basic operational functions of an accountant can often be so demanding that they could very well, as Forbes says, "smother other ingredients" of success, but if you're going to rise above the norm, you can't allow this to happen. At some point, you have to look beyond the figures and focus your energy and attention on what the figures tell you. "Nothing will hold you back more in accounting," says Buddy Martin, CPA and partner in the firm of Seymour Schneidman & Associates, "than having tunnel vision. You have to see the whole picture—not just the numbers."

ACCOMPLISHMENT
FOR THE "ART" OF IT

It should come as no surprise to learn that the overwhelming percentage of highly successful people truly love what they do. As Malcolm Forbes, who is probably the best example I know of a businessman who takes enormous pleasure in his work, likes to put it, "If you don't like what you're doing, you'll never be successful. I don't think anybody does something really well unless they truly enjoy what they do."

What's true for business people as a whole is true for accountants. But more than loving what they do, successful accountants, as a group, see an element of challenge and romance in virtually everything they do, even the most routine tasks. "It all depends on how you look at things," says Saul Silverman. "Take a job as routine as checking bills to verify accuracy. If the only thing you're interested in is accuracy, it's drudgery. But if you're looking, with interest, at bills, receipts, freight vouchers, what you're getting is a story. Then, there's more romance. You can follow what's happening."

It's a familiar theme. Some people refer to it as "sinking your teeth into a project." Others liken what *they* do for companies to what surgeons do for sick people. Malcolm Forbes calls it "enjoying the idea of digging meaning out of figures." Isaac Assael, CPA, partner in M. R. Weiser & Co., calls it "the desire for excellence." Bruce Morris, CA (chartered accountant) who heads our Vancouver office, sees it as an almost inherent need in successful accountants to have a "good feeling about themselves" and to feel confident about their training. Thomas Hurst, who spent much of his accounting career with General Motors before joining our Phoenix franchise, describes this quality as "an attitude for doing whatever you do well." Whatever it is, you always manage to feel a certain sense of excitement whenever the top people in the profession talk about accounting.

INTELLECTUAL CURIOSITY

"On my first day of class in college," recalls Harry A. Gilbert, CPA, who heads our Southern California franchise, "I had a professor who said to us, 'Everybody here will get an A in my class if you learn to apply your reasoning powers.'" Gilbert says he's never forgotten that opening-day speech and attributes the success he has enjoyed in accounting and business to the fact that he has kept that principle in mind throughout his business career.

Gilbert remembers, for instance, that soon after he graduated he joined a 40-person CPA firm whose philosophy was a reaffirmation of what his professor had said. "They preached to us at the firm that when you're through with your work papers on the job and the debits equal the credits, that is only the beginning of the job. That's when you step back and look at it and ask yourself, 'Does it make sense? Is the profit reasonable for the amount of sales that were done in that period?' In other words, what they were looking for was a test of 'reasonableness.'"

What Gilbert is talking about here is possibly the one trait, above all others, that differentiates the accountants at the top of the profession from the middle-of-the-road practitioners. "What it all comes down to," Philip B. Chenok, CPA, president of the American Institute of CPAs, told me, "is inquisitiveness. The most successful accountants I know are prone not to accept information without raising questions when things don't appear to make sense. There is an element of common sense that comes through in their assessments and evaluations."

Let me amend Chenok's statement with a brief anecdote about a highly competent accountant I once knew, who lost out on a position he wanted very badly—for the very reason we're discussing here, a lack of inquisitiveness, the inability to see beyond the numbers. The accountant had great credentials, but when the interviewer asked him to talk about his most interesting client—a small southern college—all the accountant apparently knew were the numbers. Explained the interviewer to me afterward, "When the candidate didn't tell me anything exciting about the client he'd been working with for several years, I realized I was dealing with somebody who did not have an inquiring mind and didn't have much depth, either."

SUCCESS INGREDIENTS: A SUMMARY

The qualities I've just mentioned are hardly the only qualities shared by successful accountants. I've noticed, for instance, that most of the successful accountants I know are positive thinkers. You rarely hear them complaining about their work or about the pressures they're under. Most of them have a healthy sense of humor: They take what they do seriously, but they can laugh at themselves, too. In short, while they may be single-minded about their careers, they are also well-rounded individuals who give you the impression that they would be successful in any field.

TEST YOUR AMBITION QUOTIENT

I've put together a self-test that will help you answer the question implied at the beginning of the chapter: Do you really want to be successful? I don't claim the test to be scientific, but taking it will at least give you some idea of just how ambitious you are to be successful.

To take the test, gauge the degree to which each of the statements below applies to you. Fill in each blank on a scale of 1 to 5, with 1 indicating that the statement does not apply to you at all and 5 indicating that the statement very much applies to you.

1. I truly enjoy working. _____
2. Given free time, I would rather be out socializing with people than sitting home watching television. _____
3. My first response to a problem is to try to figure out the most practical solution. _____
4. One of the things I like best about work is the challenge of it. _____
5. I believe very strongly in the work ethic. _____
6. I have a strong desire to get things done. _____
7. When there is a difficult situation, I enjoy assuming the responsibility for correcting it. _____

 8. I frequently come up with ideas—day and night. _____
 9. I'm not satisfied with the success I already enjoy. _____
10. I rarely miss a day of work because of illness. _____
11. I enjoy vacations, but after four or five days I look forward to getting back to work. _____
12. I can usually get along with six hours of sleep. _____
13. I'm interested in meeting people and developing contacts. _____
14. I set high standards for myself in almost everything I do. _____
15. All in all, I consider myself a lucky person. _____
16. I'm not afraid to rely on my instincts when I have to make an important decision. _____
17. I can think of very few situations in my life in which I do not have a great deal of control. _____
18. I recover from setbacks pretty quickly. I don't dwell on them. _____
19. I'm not afraid to admit it when I make a big mistake. _____
20. Achieving success is important to me. _____

HOW TO RATE YOURSELF

Score	Interpretation
85 to 100	Very high ambition quotient: with the proper skills, you are almost certain to achieve your goals.
70 to 84	Higher than average: your chances of achieving your ambition are very good, provided that you have the talent and skills to go along with your desire.
55 to 69	About average: if you have achieved your ambition—or are about to achieve it—it will not be because of your attitude or approach.
Below 55	Below average: success, by most people's standards, is not an important goal for you.

CHAPTER THREE **GETTING THE MOST OUT OF YOURSELF**

Brains, diligence, personality, and appearance—use any one of these properly and you'll get along. Use them all and you've got power.

A good many years ago, before I started my personnel recruiting company, I attended a daylong seminar at which one of the speakers was a prominent professor who was a tax lawyer and CPA and who was known in particular for his expertise in a specialized phase of tax law.

I was not at the time—and I'm certainly not now—an expert in taxes, but I was interested in tax law, and even as a very young man, I was a reasonably knowledgeable student on the subject. Yet I'm not embarrassed to admit that from the moment this professor began talking until he finished his presentation 45 minutes later, I was lost—and for a good reason. There was no central thought to his talk, no logical progression of ideas, no theme—just a jumble of section numbers and statements strung together in random fashion. Worse, the professor spoke in a barely audible monotone and looked out at his audience only once or twice during the speech. After he finished his talk, he didn't bother to ask if anybody had any questions.

I was disappointed. I had wanted very much to learn about what he had to say, and it troubled me that somebody who knew so much about a subject I wanted to learn more about had absolutely no idea of how to communicate this information—and didn't seem to care.

What surprised me more than anything about the speech was how tolerant the audience was. There were about 20 of us in the conference room. I was one of the few accountants—the rest were lawyers and business executives—and it was clear from the way the people were talking after the speech that I wasn't the only person in the audience who didn't understand what the speaker was trying to say. It was also clear that nobody was as upset as I. As the lawyer who had been sitting next to me during the speech put it, "What can you expect? The guy's really an accountant."

As I said, this seminar took place a good many years ago. I mention it here because the comment of the lawyer has always troubled me—mainly because I have heard it in one form or another over and over again in all the years I've been involved in the accounting profession. Unfortunately, it's a comment that reflects the image that many people have of accountants.

The image I'm talking about depicts accountants as introverts who are more comfortable with numbers than they are with people, and whose contributions to the companies they serve are confined primarily to making sure the numbers add up properly on the balance sheet. Here is how writer Mark Stevens describes this image in *The Big Eight*:

> You can spot the technicians a mile away. Just walk through the halls of The Big Eight and peek inside the offices. You'll see all kinds of men and women. Technicians are the ones who look as though they've been locked in a library since puberty. It's a strange breed: introverted, glazy-eyed little men, they dress in sober fashion even by Big Eight standards, stare at their shoes, and carry themselves with icy formality.

Granted, Mr. Stevens is generalizing here, and I surely don't mean to suggest that his description applies to the accounting profession as a whole. I know hundreds of accountants quite well, and outside of the fact that, as a group, they tend to be a little more conservative and precise than the world at large, I find it impossible to make generalizations about them. In their appearance, their personality, their outlook on life, you will find as much diversity as among other groups of professionals. Some are quiet and reserved. Others are boisterous and aggressive. Some have sedentary hobbies, like stamp collecting. Others go in for more adventurous pursuits, like skiing or mountain climbing. I know of a California accountant who races motorcycles on the weekends, although I don't think he advertises this fact to his clients.

These considerations apart, the fact remains that accountants do suffer from an image problem—particularly, I think, in management accounting. A study conceived by my company and conducted by Burke Marketing found that some corporate executives perceived management accountants as "glorified bookkeepers."

Mind you, we're not dealing here with reality, but with the way people perceive other people. And the facts are clear. The business community perceives accountants differently from the way accountants perceive themselves. I base this view on more than my personal experience. (On more occasions than I could ever count, I've had employers looking for an accountant say to me, "I don't want a 'typical' accountant. I want somebody with personality.") I base it also on the results of the Burke Marketing Research survey conducted expressly for this book. One striking feature of that survey was the difference between the way accountants perceive themselves and the way other business people perceive accountants.

For example, when we asked respondents to specify the degree to which they agreed with the statement, "Public accountants have the ability to get along well with people," some 41 percent of CPA partners answered "very strongly." When the same question was put to top corporate management, only 10 percent agreed "very strongly"—a difference of some 30 percentage points. And when personnel directors were asked how strongly they agreed with the statement, only 14 percent answered "very strongly."

The poll turned up a similar divergence of views on the subject of communication skills. About 45 percent of the CPA partners we queried agreed "strongly" with the statement that "Public accountants have good communications skills," but only 14 percent of corporate personnel directors shared this feeling, and only 6 percent of top corporate management felt that accountants have good communication skills.

In the case of management accountants, the divergence we found was not as striking. In general, however, the financial people we spoke to—

the chief financial officers and the CPA partners—had a higher opinion of management accountants than the nonfinancial people.

What do these figures tell us? In short, they tell us that in certain key areas—communications and interpersonal relations, to cite just two—there is a fundamental and crucial gap between the way accountants, particularly public accountants, perceive themselves and the way they are perceived by top management. They also tell us that if you're interested in getting ahead in accounting, a good place to start is with the image you project to the rest of the world.

IMAGE: IT STARTS WITH YOUR APPEARANCE

Years ago, I had a morning meeting with a financial executive of a large industrial company, at the end of which I observed something I've never forgotten. The executive excused himself from his office and came back moments later with a change of clothing. Throughout the morning he'd been wearing a light-colored plain suit. Now he was wearing a dark pinstripe. Why did he change clothes? His luncheon date that afternoon was with a Boston banker!

For better or worse, all of us are judged—to some degree at least—by our appearance. And whether we want to admit it or not, most of us base our own judgments on appearance too. True, once we get to know somebody well, our impressions become based on more meaningful criteria, but the problem in business is that many of the people we deal with we will see only now and then. This is particularly the case, I think, with accountants. If you're working for a CPA firm, for instance, you probably see many clients three or four times a year, so you need to ask yourself whether or not you are making a strong enough and favorable enough impression. As Patricia Frechtman, a personnel management consultant, says, "You never get a second chance to make a good first impression."

We know, from psychological studies, some of the judgments that people are likely to make on the basis of appearance. Studies by psychologist Ellen Berscheid, an expert in the psychology of attractiveness, show that if someone considers you attractive they are also likely to consider you kind, genuine, sincere, and interesting. Another set of studies has shown that if you are a male executive who stands over 6 feet 2 inches tall, you probably earn a 12 percent higher salary than a man under 6 feet. In one of the most interesting studies done on the subject, it was found that panhandlers who are reasonably well dressed will get more than shabbily dressed panhandlers.

Granted, not everybody can look like a movie star, and your height is something you really can't do anything about. But there are many aspects of your appearance over which you have a great deal of control. I'm talking, in particular, about the way you dress, the way you carry yourself, the way you speak: in short, the image you generate whenever you're with other people. Observes Frank M. Davidson, a Harvard MBA and CPA who heads our northwestern franchises, "As basic as it may seem, the general image you project is one of the things that a great many accountants simply overlook."

The relationship between the image you project and career success in business is such that more than 100 companies nationwide specialize in telling businessmen and businesswomen how to get the most out of their appearance. So, perhaps not to you, but certainly to the people you have to deal with in your job, appearance *does* count. For this reason alone, you should do everything in your power to look as good as you possibly can.

HOW YOU DRESS

Most accountants, in my experience, simply do not give enough thought to their business wardrobes. Yet this is one aspect of your appearance over which you can exercise a great deal of control. Dress requirements vary according to the sort of firm you work for and region of the country in which you live, but in most cases, you'll be expected to dress in as conservative and businesslike a style as possible. Most firms like to see their men in dark, traditionally styled suits and their women in tailored suits and dresses.

The reasons are obvious. "It isn't just for *our* sake that we are very concerned about the appearance of our accountants," says Robert Maynard, CPA, a partner and national director of human resources for Price Waterhouse. "We have to think about the reactions our clients are going to have to somebody who wears a rumpled suit and looks scraggly. Appearance is one of the things we look at very carefully when we hire candidates."

Regardless of the guidelines that prevail in your firm, however, the basic rule for you to keep in mind is this: Everything in your wardrobe should in one way or another *enhance* your image. Everything you wear, in other words, should make you appear substantial, educated, trustworthy, confident—all the qualities you need for success.

I suggest, to begin with, that you set aside some time soon to go through your clothes closet. As you do, look through every piece of clothing you wear when you're at work. At the same time, ask yourself whether that piece of clothing, whether it's a shirt, a blouse, a suit, a tie, or a pair of shoes, is doing anything to enhance your image as a professional. Then think to yourself how you *feel* when you wear this item. Do you feel comfortable and important? I know a highly successful accountant who spends more than $500 for his suits. When somebody suggested that he might look just as good in a $250 suit, he replied, "Yes, but I wouldn't *feel* as good."

In the event you don't have a sense of what clothes suit you best, I suggest one of two things: (1) Find a clothing store with an excellent reputation for conservative clothes and put yourself in its hands. (2) Buy one of the several books out on the market today that talk about business dress. None of these books is written specifically for accountants, but each gives advice that applies to professional people in general. One of the things these books will preach to you is that it's better to have a few high-quality clothing items than a closet full of bargain basement specials. Tailoring, in particular, is crucial. That's why, if you have an unusual build, you are almost always better off having your clothes made to order than you are buying them ready-made.

This brings up the cardinal rule of dressing: designing your wardrobe around your build and coloring. If you're on the heavy side, stick with darker colors—they'll give you a thinner appearance. If you're on the short and stocky side, you should choose pinstripes and, at all costs, keep away from plaid sports jackets and slacks. They widen your appearance. If you have a pale complexion, don't dress in anything too dark: It will merely accentuate your pallor.

As far as styles go, single-breasted suits are fine for average-sized men, but I've noticed that a lot of the taller men in accounting favor dark, double-breasted suits.

For women, the guidelines are just as specific. Advises Patricia Frechtman, "A tailored suit, nicely cut, in a soft blue, gray, or brown material always looks businesslike. Most professional women prefer to wear a blouse with either a button-down collar and a silk tie or one with its own bow that ties softly at the neck. Footwear should be simple, comfortable pumps."

Patricia Frechtman goes on to advise that where jewelry is concerned, a woman is always better off with too little than too much. "Plain gold jewelry or pearls are always in good taste," she says, "but avoid clinking bracelets or flashy dinner rings." She also warns against wearing see-through blouses, low necklines, and tight-fitting skirts with slits. "Remember," she says, "if you want to be treated as a professional, you have to look like a professional."

BEYOND YOUR WARDROBE

Your appearance, of course, involves more than what you wear. You can spend a small fortune on your wardrobe, but your appearance will still suffer if you neglect your grooming, your complexion, and your general physical shape, and, if you're a woman, if you're not careful with your makeup. Let's look at a few guidelines.

Your Face

The main thing to be said about your facial appearance is that you should be comfortable with the way you look. To be sure, you don't have to look like a movie star to move ahead in accounting, but at the same time you don't want your facial appearance to interfere with your career progress.

As you undoubtedly know, more and more executives these days— male and female alike—are going in for cosmetic surgery—face-lifts and surgery around the eyes in particular. Their rationale is that looking better—and younger—gives them more confidence and enables them to function more effectively at their jobs. My own feeling about cosmetic surgery—and it's a feeling shared by many people who counsel executives on how to look better—is that you should seek it only when there is something about your physical appearance that is a major source of embarrassment or discomfort to you.

What I *do* advocate, though, is that you pay close attention to your teeth, for if there is anything you want to feel confident about, it's your smile. A rising executive at one of the major CPA firms was unhappy and stymied by the gaps between his teeth. He spent a great deal of money to have his front teeth capped and insists to this day that his rise in the firm since the dental work was done has more than paid for the investment.

What about makeup? "The rule, again," says Patricia Frechtman, "is less is better than more. Some women today wear far too much makeup while others, primarily younger women, shun makeup altogether. I suggest a happy medium. Cosmetics, when used properly, enhance a woman's best features and hide her worst." She also suggests that women who may not be confident about makeup seek the help of a professional. "In any department store across the country," she says, "there are trained personnel who will help you make the most of your makeup."

Your Hair

Numerous studies have shown that your hair affects the image people have of you as much as anything else about your appearance. Many people, for instance, automatically associate a slick-backed look with criminal activity. Others look at wild and unruly hair and immediately think of instability. Still others will look at a man with a severe crew cut and assume that he must have been a Marine. Are these judgments accurate? Of course not. But they exist, and you have to live with them.

Whatever hairstyle you choose, make sure it's one that works best for your features and your type of hair. Don't be hesitant about spending a few extra dollars for a barber or a stylist who can give you the best look. Needless to say, your hair should always be clean and free of dandruff.

I should mention something about hairpieces for men if only to press my position that you are almost always better off avoiding them. In the first place, all but the most expensive hairpieces—the ones that can cost several thousand dollars—almost invariably appear artificial. Second, hairpieces can be distracting, and some people tend to stop concentrating on the man they're talking to and pay more attention to the hairpiece.

As far as women go, I'll yield again to Frechtman, who stresses the importance of a natural hairstyle that requires little upkeep. "Your hair shouldn't hang down in your eyes or cover your face," she says. "And if you're wearing hair combs, they should be simple, and their color should blend with your hair. If your color is *not* your natural color, make sure you have a regular appointment for coloring."

She gives a final piece of advice to women on the subject of hair. "Don't play with your hair," she says. "Many women do this when they're nervous, and it's a distracting habit. The best way to avoid the habit is to have well-groomed hair that stays in place and does nothing that might detract from your image."

On now to moustaches and beards, which are touchy subjects in many firms. I know of accountants who've grown beards in order to appear wiser, but I know just as many accounting partners who see beards as a sign of nonconformity and do not encourage beards among junior staff members. Moustaches, on the other hand, have a somewhat higher rate of acceptance in the older, larger firms. Still, if I were a young accountant looking to generate a winning image in today's market, I would wear neither a moustache nor a beard, unless I wanted to conceal a scar or other facial defect. My philosophy in business has always been to play the odds: When something can't do me any good, there is always the chance that it will do me harm. Why gamble?

Don't Forget Your Nails

There isn't too much to be said about the appearance and condition of your nails, but the little bit that needs to be said is nonetheless important, particularly for men. Unlike women, for whom nail care is one of the basics of good grooming, many men are unaware of the degree to which poorly cared for nails can take away from one's appearance.

Basic nail care for men consists of making sure your nails are always clean and well shaped and that your cuticles are pushed back and trimmed. An inexpensive nailbrush is all you need to keep your nails clean, but you should spend a little extra to buy a basic nail kit—nail clipper, cuticle scissors, nail file—for weekly self-maintenance. I would also recommend that you get a manicure (although without polish), not only for the appearance of your nails but for the basic conditioning that a good manicure provides. Women should not wear their nails too long, should not use too bright a polish, and should *never* get caught with chipped polish. A small bottle of polish remover is probably a better safeguard than polish used to patch up a chip.

Your Physical Shape

Nobody expects you to be built like Clint Eastwood or Jane Fonda, but most of the highly successful accountants I know radiate a sense of fitness and energy and any number of studies indicate that the kind of physical shape you're in has a direct bearing on your career progress.

We have found over and over again in our own studies, for instance, that all things being equal, an obese person is much less likely to be hired than a nonobese person. I'm not saying there aren't accounting partners who couldn't stand to take off 20 pounds, but I'm willing to bet that if you surveyed the leading partners in the top 20 accounting firms throughout the country, you would find that relatively few of them are substantially overweight and that most of them do something—whether it's jogging, swimming, or walking—to keep trim. Says Charles J. Wolff, CPA, who owns our Phoenix office, "If you neglect your health and appearance in accounting, you're sabotaging your career. And one of the best things any accountant who isn't already exercising can do is to get into some regular fitness activity."

Apart from what it does to enhance your appearance and your health, a regular fitness activity, whether it is swimming, tennis, squash, or running, gives you a built-in means of expanding your contacts and of dealing with the pressures that are inherent in accounting. "The one thing I regret," says Saul Silverman, "is that I stopped taking part in sports as soon as I got busy in my career. I see now that if I had played, say, tennis or golf I could have benefited in many ways. I would have had an activity I enjoyed, and I would have met more people. One of the best things an accountant, man or woman, can do today is to become involved in some sport."

YOUR IMAGE: OTHER CONSIDERATIONS

Your appearance encompasses factors that go beyond the way you look and dress. Recently, for instance, I saw a job application from an accountant who had been working for one of the best-known CPA firms but had been fired. The reason, according to the application: "I drove a pickup."

Firing an accountant because he drives a pickup truck may seem harsh. Then again, think about it. If you headed a $100 million company, would you be comfortable with an accountant who came to see you in a pickup truck? I doubt it. So don't overlook the little things. The car you drive, the kind of stationery you use, the design of your business card, the message you put on your telephone answering machine—all of it contributes to your image, and none of it should be taken for granted.

In this regard, I would suggest that if you—or your company—can afford it, you should travel first class. This may sound extravagant to you, but there are some sound reasons for flying first class, apart from the added comfort of the flight. First of all, traveling first class massages your ego: When you *think* you're important, you *become* important. Second, the added room you have in first class makes it easier for you to catch up on your paperwork when you're traveling.

But probably the key advantage of traveling first class over tourist is that you stand a good chance of meeting business people who could become clients or valuable contacts in the future. While flying first class, I have met any number of people who were in a position to give our company business. One of them, the executive vice president of a leading Pittsburgh corporation, has given our franchise there a great deal of business over a long period of time.

The last time I flew to Europe, I flew the Concorde. While waiting for the plane in the Concorde lounge at Heathrow, I met an executive from one of the leading industrial firms in England, whose firm just happened to need financial people for its headquarters in London and its affiliate in Hong Kong. I'm sure our British people will be hearing from that firm.

Mind you, I never actively solicit business—and neither should you. If I meet someone who doesn't ask me what I do, I'm content to talk about the weather or the news of the day. But when you're sitting next to someone on a flight that's longer than a few hours, chances are the conversation is eventually going to come around to business.

The same principle holds true for hotels and restaurants. If you're visiting an out-of-town client, you want the hotel you stay at to reflect an image of success. Again, there is a cost factor to consider, but the difference between the truly first-rate hotels and the typical business person's hotel usually isn't that great and seems to me to be well worth the difference. Most of the most successful executives I know have become regular customers at a handful of very good restaurants and will go to those restaurants when they're entertaining. When you're out of town, it's not as easy to become known at the better restaurants, but you might consider dropping by the restaurant in person to make your reservation, to choose the table you want, and to give the maître d'hôtel your card—along with a tip. One more thing to think about when you're taking clients out to dinner and you're driving a car is to tip the parking attendant a little extra in advance in order to get a spot that will enable you to get your car immediately.

DEVELOPING YOUR INTERPERSONAL SKILLS

As it happens, our Burke findings do not paint all that bleak a picture of an accountant's interpersonal skills. Except for the fact that 30 percent of top management had negative things to say about the interpersonal skills of their internal accountants, the general feeling as it emerged from our Burke survey was that accountants are neither here nor there when it comes to the ability to get along well with people, which makes an accountant who can combine interpersonal skills with technical competence an accountant with a rosy future.

"We've had many absolutely brilliant people working for us, and we still do," says Richard Hickok. "The brilliant ones who have not met with success simply did not know how to get along well with clients. As an example, we once sent an accountant to work with the payroll manager of a client, and the accountant was so arrogant he made the payroll manager appear stupid. We quickly got a call from the client telling us to take the accountant off that job. That kind of a track record is not going to get an accountant very far in this profession."

Denis J. O'Leary, CPA, the director of personnel of Main Hurdman, feels much the same way as Hickok. "Technical skills are most important during the first five or six years of your career," he says, "but after that time, progress depends largely on how well you relate to people: how you relate to the people above you, how well you supervise, how well you're able to deal with the client and the client's personnel—in short, your ability to communicate with all people. That's where we draw the distinction between the accountants who are going to move forward versus the ones who are not going any further. Technical requirements are always going to be necessary, but as you move up, the interpersonal skills take on more and more importance."

To be sure, there is nothing complicated about interpersonal skills. "Skills," in fact, is a misleading word, since it implies that getting along well with people is something you learn, like a course in advanced math. Basically, it's a matter of being courteous, pleasant, and understanding in your dealings with other people. It's *caring* genuinely about other people—being sensitive to their feelings. It means being tactful when you are pointing out a mistake to a secretary, and being patient and understanding if, say, a company auditor hasn't put together the figures you're looking for.

It is also recognizing that regardless of the situation, your best interests are rarely served if you have to resort to tactics that irritate people. "More often than most accountants realize," says Graham Thompson, CA, in charge of our Calgary franchise, "accountants with personalities that grate on others are their own worst enemies. They don't realize that when their personality grates on others, they get frozen out of information and gradually they begin to lose authority."

I have my own theory about why some accountants have a difficult time getting along with people, and it has to do with the kind of training accountants receive. As an accountant, you're trained to be inquisitive, almost to the point of being suspicious. You're trained to look for oversights, deceptions—even frauds. Some accountants, however, let this suspiciousness carry over into other areas of their work. Their suspicions prevent them from communicating well and from delegating. (Some accountants are suspicious of subordinates they themselves have hired.) I might add, too, that unless accountants can keep this tendency to be suspicious from taking over their personalities, their overall performance suffers.

There are two interpersonal skills I'd like to mention here, primarily because they are qualities that many people overlook. The first is being a good listener. The second is having a sense of humor. As you probably know, most people are not very good at listening, and the reason, psychologists tell us, is that listening isn't as easy as most people think. The average person, for instance, speaks at a rate of about 125 words per minute, but most of us think at the rate of 400 to 500 words per minute, and we can listen at the speed of 600 words per minute. As a result, the natural tendency of the listener is to let the mind stray. Another problem with listening is that many people, instead of listening to what is being said to them, tend to think about what they're going to say next. This would explain an observation of mine that ears are so sensitive they sometimes hear things that are never said.

Psychologists insist that the only way to improve your listening skills is to concentrate on them. You have to resist the natural tendency of your mind to drift, and you must resist the temptation to concentrate on your reply. You have to think about it, concentrate on it and, most of all, care about it.

As far as a sense of humor goes, it should suffice to say that even as an accountant, you're entitled to have one, and that in many situations having a sense of humor can be the difference in your ability to get through difficult situations. "A sense of humor is particularly important for women," says Caryn Newman, a CPA who is now a financial executive for a department store chain. "I can remember any number of occasions in which a receptionist had trouble accepting the fact that I was really an accountant. When I was a public accountant, I once went to a television station client and was asked by the receptionist if I was the 'talent' for the talk show. Sure, it's easy to get disturbed in that kind of a situation, but what would it gain me?"

All told, then, developing interpersonal skills requires little skill in and of itself, but it does require a great deal of practice. It's mostly a matter of making the effort to get along with the people you deal with. Here are a few guidelines, some of them perhaps obvious, but all of them important:

1. Smile at people when you first meet them.
2. Look them in the eye (but don't overdo it).
3. Don't work too hard to make a good impression.
4. Don't talk too much about yourself—show an interest in others.
5. Make it a point to listen to what people are saying to you (rather than thinking up your reply).
6. Show courtesy to everyone.
7. Have a sense of humor.

SHARPENING THE WAY YOU COMMUNICATE

As I mentioned earlier, only 6 percent of the top management personnel we queried in our Burke study gave high marks to the communication skills of public accountants, and only 8 percent of top management felt that the communication skills of management accountants were particularly strong.

Considering the fact that we're talking about the most basic of management skills, I find these figures significant, particularly since most of the accountants also made mention of the weaknesses that many accountants have in communication skills and stressed that these weaknesses were interfering with their careers. "The accountants I've known who have difficulty moving up," says Michael Goldstein, "are weak in two major skills—their interpersonal skills and their communication skills. And these are the two skills that are simply not taught at an accounting school."

The pity of all this is that speaking and writing are skills that are easily learned, provided you make the commitment to learn them. Many of the large public accounting firms and corporations, for instance, offer courses in both skills, and in almost every city there are seminars that teach the basic techniques. Some of these speaking seminars, for instance, give you the chance to see yourself on video as you learn to control your nervousness, make better eye contact with your audience, and use your voice to better advantage. The better writing seminars, on the other hand, can teach you how to be more efficient in your overall approach to writing and how to write what you want to say simply and directly.

The value of developing each of these skills cannot be overstated. For instance, our Burke survey showed that 96 percent of CPA partners and 94 percent of chief financial officers (CFOs) felt that it was easier for articulate accountants to get ahead in public accounting, and 100 percent of top corporate management had the same thing to say about management accountants who are articulate. Also, the ability to communicate well in speaking and writing will make you that much more effective as a manager. (By the same token, weaknesses in either of these skills will limit your effectiveness as a manager.)

Once you gain some confidence in your ability to speak, you might want to start giving talks to local groups and in this way gain the kind of recognition that will almost invariably advance your career. You might talk about taxes, money management, business, finance—any number of things. Keep in mind that you do not have to be a professional speaker in order to be sought out by organizations to talk on these subjects. As long as you know your material and can deliver it in a personable, confident, and reasonably interesting way, you'll be in demand. People do not expect to be entertained by an accountant. They come for information.

The same principle holds true for writing. Robert Randall, the managing editor of *Management Accounting* magazine, tells me that he knows of a number of cases in which accountants were offered good jobs after their articles appeared in his magazine. "The pattern of success I've seen," he says, "is with those accountants who are the most articulate in their speaking and writing abilities. It's relatively easy for a firm to get a good technician, but you can't buy the other attributes."

Here, again, you don't have to be an accomplished essayist to get an article published in a magazine. You simply have to know your material and be able to express yourself in clear, direct English. The magazine will handle the editing.

I'll have more to say on speaking and writing as important tools for marketing yourself in Chapter Seven. For now, it's enough to recognize that of all the skills you develop, few will do more to enhance your career progress than the ability to communicate effectively.

BECOME AN AUTHORITY

No matter what else your personality projects about you, people should perceive you as an authority, particularly when it comes to matters of accounting and finance. Regardless of what your job may be, you should be able to discuss such topics as economics and inflation intelligently. You should know something about business conditions in general. People expect that much from an accountant, and if you don't demonstrate this knowledge, you won't inspire confidence.

The best way to become an authority, of course, is to read. If you're not doing so already, you should be subscribing to many of the major business publications, such as *The Wall Street Journal, Forbes, Business Week,* and *Fortune* and to the major accounting journals, such as the *Journal of Accounting, Management Accounting,* and *The Practical Accountant.* If I were you, I would also subscribe to the newsletters relating to your specific specialty. Set aside at least an hour each day in order to read (but don't do it at work). You want to be able to discuss matters with your colleagues and your superiors. You should be able to read quickly. If you're a slow reader, take a speed-reading course. You might also want to consider using a highlight pen to call your attention to important thoughts and ideas.

In my career, I have found it extremely useful to keep a permanent clipping file of articles, reports, and any general information that is related to my business. I started this "morgue"—the newspaper term for a permanent file—more than 30 years ago, and it has grown to more than half a dozen or so large filing cabinets. I collect anything I can get my hands on that has to do with hiring or managing people. I even collect appropriate humor.

Some of my friends tell me I overdo these things, and maybe I do. On the other hand, whenever I have had to prepare a speech or give testimony before a congressional committee, write an article, or appear on radio or TV, I have never been at a loss for relevant data. It gives me a kick, too, that reporters and authors ask me to check my file for material on subjects they are writing about. The fact that I'm happy to oblige makes them that much more cooperative when it comes to supporting my company's public relations.

Apart from becoming an authority on the subjects that relate to accounting, I recommend strongly that you develop and cultivate an interest in a field or area that has nothing to do with accounting—something you enjoy that could also enhance your career prospects.

Consider Dan G. Kramer, CPA, who has been the managing editor of the *CPA Journal* for 10 years. For 23 years before becoming an editor, he was a partner at Oppenheim, Appel, Dixon & Co. Kramer has always loved classical music and at Oppenheim found himself developing a broad variety of music clients. "I'm not saying," Kramer explained to me, "that my interest in music created this business for our firm, but it did enable me to capitalize on it once the opportunity presented itself. I was able to talk with music people. They were comfortable with me. That's why I've always urged accountants to develop a broad variety of interests. It can't help but have some influence on an accounting career."

On the subject of becoming an authority, I would urge you, in the event you've neglected it, to become proficient at two of the most basic skills an accountant can have: The first is bookkeeping; the second is basic math. The reason being proficient at bookkeeping is so important, even in this age of the computer, is that somehow, somewhere, you're going to be involved, as an accountant, with a bookkeeper, and the last thing you want to do is embarrass yourself by calling attention to a "mistake" when there is none. It happened to me once, early in my career, and I've never forgotten it.

Then there is proficiency in math. It constantly surprises me that many accountants are not particularly good mathematicians. I know that I myself am not a crackerjack mathematician, but I have worked hard at it, and I've become a little better than adequate. Today, with calculators a basic tool in the industry, it's gettng harder and harder to find young accountants who can do simple addition, subtraction, division, and multiplication without the calculator.

Wouldn't you agree that an accountant creates a better impression by doing basic calculations rapidly and without a machine? Don't you think that if you're in a restaurant or are buying something in a store, the people with you will be favorably impressed when they see how quickly and accurately you can audit the bill? The reality is that you don't need to be a great mathematician to be an accountant, but the public doesn't always perceive things that way.

GET TO KNOW THE COMPUTER

You don't have to be a computer expert to know that most business functions today are being computerized, especially in accounting. A number of firms, among them Main Hurdman, are even beginning to send auditors equipped with portable computers to their clients. A recent AICPA survey indicates that the number of CPA firms using computers has increased tenfold since 1981, as compared with only a twofold increase from 1974 to 1981. Citing again from our Burke survey, we found that virtually everyone we queried—nearly 95 percent—recognized the importance of having some knowledge of the computer. Interestingly, CPA partners and CFOs found knowing the computer more important for management accountants than for public accountants.

The computer has freed accounting firms from much of the computational drudgery that used to be so much a part of the day-to-day routine in accounting. This has enabled the profession to become a good deal more sophisticated and accountants to broaden the scope of their services to clients—to do more analyzing and consulting. The reason is that so much financial planning today is done with computers, and in public accounting, the computer is so important that some firms now have computers to audit the computers.

When I talk about learning the computer, I'm talking about two things: one, learning the basic principles of computer sciences, such as language; and, two, learning how to operate microcomputers and minicomputers. The idea in each case should be to gain knowledge about computers and what they do so that you can take an active role in your firm's computer operations.

Another skill you might have to learn as part of your computer education, in the event that you haven't already learned it, is typing. Curiously enough, it is their inability to type that is keeping many executives from using computer terminals, but accountants cannot afford this kind of resistance. If it is of any consolation to you, typing, if you apply yourself, is not difficult to learn.

In any case, becoming comfortable with the computer will take a commitment. Alex Cohen, a CPA and attorney who is the publisher of *The Practical Accountant*, estimates that it takes about a year to learn the basics of computer science. He recommends not only buying a home computer but reading the computer journals, attending trade shows, and taking computer courses. I think it's a good idea for accountants to make the computer their hobby. Working with a home computer can be as much fun as chess, bridge, coin collecting, or music, and it will have a direct bearing on your performance at work. You could set up home programs to monitor your investment, or you could try to set up programs that relate specifically to your firm's operations.

Equally important, if it's possible, is to get involved as much as possible whenever there is going to be a computer installation or revision in your firm. Michael Goldstein did this in the early 1970s when a firm he was with decided to put in a computer, and Goldstein insists that his knowledge of computers was one of the principle factors in his rise to managing partner with Laventhal & Horwath.

The point is, as computers become more and more a fixture in American businesses, management is going to have to rely more and more on accountants to become resident experts. Don't get left out.

BUILD A CONTACT CLUB

It's axiomatic that nobody gets to the top, or even near the top, without help from other people. Indeed, I can think of several successful people, not only in accounting but in other fields, whose chief ability, really, is the ability to capitalize on the people they know. They're not "using people" in the way you normally interpret the phrase. They not only rely on others for help and favors, they give a great deal of help and do favors themselves. That's an important reason they're successful. "In the end, it comes down to having an interest in people," says Dan Kramer. "A partner of Oppenheim used to say that if you multiplied the number of friends you had before you were 40 by a certain factor, you could probably estimate how successful you're going to be. The idea was that friends, aside from their important life values, are likely to be the best sources of business."

I consider building contacts so basic to career success that you should be systematic about it. Whenever you meet somebody new, you should write that person's name and business on a 3 × 5 file card or, better still, use your personal computer. If you both feel that you are in a position to help each other, try to meet socially. If you're in a position to help the person, try to do it early in the relationship. It will then be much easier for you to go to that person if you need a favor in the future. It is particularly important for you to build contacts in the company for which you work. It's not necessary to force yourself on anyone, but don't be timid about introducing yourself to top management in the appropriate situation.

What it's called today is networking, and one accountant who has a lot to say on the subject is William Aiken, a partner in Main Hurdman, who stresses the importance of *giving* as well as taking from the network. "What I tell the young professionals," says Aiken, "is that a network is like investing in securities. If you keep taking from the principal investment, eventually there will nothing there to generate interest." So you can't just take. You have to keep investing in the network, helping people.

Aiken stresses, too, the importance of not only cultivating contacts but of making sure that you don't abuse the relationship by making it too one-sided. "In networking," he says, "the worst thing you can do is to get into a pattern in which the only time you're calling on people is when you need a favor from them. You have to keep in contact with people even when things are going well."

REMEMBER, YOU'RE A PROFESSIONAL

Accounting, by its very nature, calls for confidentiality and integrity. Should the people you work with, or for, begin to doubt your ability to keep sensitive information confidential, you will find your horizons extremely limited. I don't hesitate to say that whatever else you do in your job, you must earn and maintain the image of professionalism, honesty, and trustworthiness. An accountant without these qualities is like an athlete without reflexes.

You demonstrate these qualities in any number of ways. For instance, you should make it a cardinal rule never to gossip either about your clients or your firm, regardless of how interesting the information you have might be to other people and of how "harmless" you might think the information is. I can't tell you how often I have seen accountants get themselves into trouble with loose conversation about a company they happen to be working for or a client they are auditing. In all firms, there's a written or unwritten rule that you don't talk about company business outside the shop. Yes, you can discuss economics or taxes or any number of general topics, but when it comes to inside information, the rule is very simple. You simply don't talk about it.

There is an even more practical reason for being careful about confidentiality. As an accountant, you come across a great deal of confidential information. If you can demonstrate early in your career that you can be trusted with that information, you'll be entrusted with more; and the more confidential information you have in your mental bank, the stronger your position will be to come up with suggestions and recommendations.

Beyond confidentiality, there is the question of ethics—a question that is more important today in accounting than ever before, given the problems the accounting profession went through during the 1960s and early 1970s. Because lawsuits against firms are on the increase, companies of all sizes are policing themselves far more vigorously than ever before, and good firms have little patience with employees whose ethics are dubious.

Ethical problems can arise in a number of ways. Usually, though, when accountants find themselves in an ethical dilemma, it's because of a situation they did not create. One accountant I interviewed recalled a controllership position he once held in a company whose president made it a practice of reporting account receivables to the bank on sales that had not yet been booked. "The company had cash flow problems," explained the controller, "and this was the president's way of getting additional loans from the bank. The trouble in this situation was that my signature was on the line."

The controller in this instance did what any ethical—and intelligent—accountant would have done in the same situation. He recognized that putting his signature on a false report not only was unethical but also could have a serious impact on his career. So he told the president he wasn't going to take part in this financial charade anymore. Predictably, the controller was forced to quit his job, and, predictably, the company eventually went out of business. The controller, by the way, has become quite successful.

I recall another situation that a chief financial officer from a public company in the midwest told me about. The CFO was there only a short time when the chairman of the board called him in and told him the way a 10Q was to be prepared for the SEC. The company was contemplating a merger, and the chairman wanted the records to look better. The CFO refused and was fired, but here again, by protecting his own integrity, this executive made the right career move. The merger did take place, but none of the executives in the company was retained after the merger. What's more, there were a number of investigations following the merger. In the meantime, we managed to get the CFO a better job—a job he still has—with a far better company.

The message here is clear. As an accountant, you cannot afford even the slightest of indiscretions, for it takes very little in the way of loss of trust to shatter a career. I've known of CPAs who've lost their licenses not because they were dishonest, but because they used poor judgment, and sometimes the motivation was merely to help a friend. Don't make the same mistake.

CHAPTER FOUR GETTING ON THE RIGHT CAREER PATH

Planning doesn't necessarily make things happen, but it certainly encourages things to happen.

Career planning is one of those concepts that looks wonderful on paper. First, you establish an objective—what you want to achieve in your professional career. Then you set up a plan that outlines the steps designed to lead you to this objective. You build in some means of measuring your progress. Finally, you set up some sort of contingency plan.

No doubt there are successful accountants today whose careers typify the kind of planning I've described—accountants who knew early what they wanted to do and then went on to achieve their objectives according to the timetable they had established. However, most of the successful accountants I know of have had careers that, in retrospect, do not fall into such a tidy pattern.

I know successful accountants who started in public accounting, moved into management accounting, moved back into public accounting, and ended up going out on their own. I know successful accountants who started in public accounting convinced they would be there for only a few years and wound up 20 years later as managing partner in the firm. I know successful management accountants who are still with the firm they entered 20 years ago. I know successful management accountants who have changed firms every 3 or 4 years over the past 20 years. I know of a partner in a major firm who left accounting in order to sell insurance for 4 years, only to return to public accounting. Finally, I know any number of accountants who became successful by getting *out* of accounting.

Does this mean that I consider a career plan a waste of time? Hardly! Having some sort of career plan, obviously, is as important in accounting as it is in any profession. In fact, a survey among high-ranking financial officers at Minnesota-based corporations, conducted by Charles L. Squires, vice-president of Robert Half of Minnesota, showed that more than 80 percent of the corporate officers polled considered it important for a financial executive to have a career plan. Interestingly enough, only 52 percent of the officers queried said that they themselves had followed career plans. "What this obviously means," observes Squires, "is that experience has apparently convinced the officers who have a career plan the value of it."

What do I mean by career plan? Nothing complicated, to be sure. Having a career plan means having a reasonably specific idea of where you eventually want your career to take you and how you intend to get there. Having such a plan, I should quickly point out, doesn't necessarily mean being locked into that plan and never deviating from it. But without such a plan, you're in much the same boat as someone trying to build a house without blueprints.

What's more, career planning is not something you do once and forget about. It is something you monitor throughout your career. "In advancing a career," advises one observer of the profession, "you have to be able to recognize how each phase of a career connects to each other phase. The best way to think of a career is a little like a novel, with each chapter connecting to the other." Harry Gilbert, our Los Angeles area franchisee, puts the same thought a different way. "On each change of job," he said, "you should ask yourself the question, 'Will the new job prepare me for the ones that may follow?' "

CAREER PLANNING: SOME
GENERAL THOUGHTS

I am going to assume that your primary career goals in accounting are twofold: You want to make enough money to give you financial security, and then some. At the same time, you want to derive a sense of fulfillment from what you're doing. To be sure, you can achieve these twofold objectives in any number of ways in accounting—as a partner in public accounting; as a chief financial officer or the chief executive officer of a corporation; as an executive accountant in government; as a public accountant in your own practice; or, finally, in a business in which you are not really working as an accountant but rather using your accounting knowledge, which, as all accountants know, is an excellent foundation for success in any business.

In my own case, early in my accounting career I recognized that while I considered myself a competent accountant and enjoyed the work, I took more pleasure in business than in accounting. But that's me. I know of many highly successful accountants who would never dream of leaving accounting itself. Judging by the success they've enjoyed, they've obviously made the right decisions for themselves. That's a key point: you should make the career plans that truly reflect what *you* want.

To make such decisions, you have to know yourself. You have to know what you want out of accounting, what you're willing to do in order to reach that objective, and, finally, whether you have (or can develop) the skills and personal traits required to achieve this objective.

I cannot tell you what you want and can do. I *can*, however, ask you some questions. Your answers should give you a brief idea, at least, of whether your career has a plan to it or not.

1. *Do you have a career plan?* Have you established a specific career goal and a general strategy for reaching that goal? If not, you run the risk of drifting from job to job without building toward anything.
2. *Is your goal a realistic one?* Have you taken the time to evaluate realistically your chances of achieving your goal? For instance, if your goal is to set up your own practice, do you have the contacts—and the money—you'll need to go out on your own?
3. *Are you following your plan?* Is your present position on the career path leading to your goal? If not, is it leading to a position that will bring you closer to your goal? If you're not following your career plan, is there a logical reason?
4. *How satisfied are you with your present job?* Do you have the responsibility and are you receiving the salary you think you deserve? If not, are you in a position to do anything about it.
5. *Are you satisfied with your pattern of progress in your present company?*

Relative to others in your company, how would you assess your advancement rate? If you're moving forward in your present job, your career plan is probably moving as well.

If you answered "yes" to all of the questions above, chances are that your career path is on target. Each "no" answer, on the other hand, indicates the possibility of a detour. You would do well to examine the reasons for the "no" answer and to think about what steps you might take to deal with the problem.

CAREER PLANNING: EARLY DECISIONS

Many accountants who are looking for career success have their early decisions made for them. Because being a CPA is an important credential for career advancement in both public and private firms and in many states the only way you can qualify to be certified is to get CPA firm experience, you're most likely going to start with a CPA firm. This is true whether your long-term career goals are in public accounting or in management accounting. Most of you reading this have probably long passed this stage of your career, but some of you may still be in college, in which case the decision lies in front of you: Which type of firm is best to start with: a large, well-known national firm, or a small to medium-sized local firm?

Conventional wisdom holds that if you do get recruited out of college by one of the national firms, you should consider yourself lucky and take the job, regardless of whether your career goals lie in public accounting or in management accounting. However, our Burke survey of chief financial officers and CPA partners turned up an interesting finding: Given a choice between "getting as much varied experience as possible" or "going with a big national firm," many more chief financial officers and CPA partners recommended the former.

Not that there is a clear-cut choice between the two. The larger, better known firms do offer more prestige and usually pay better *starting* salaries. Generally, too, when you're working for a very large firm—certainly at the beginning of your career—you don't have to concern yourself too much with client development, although as competition keeps heating up in accounting, even the larger firms are going to have to concern themselves more with staff assistance in client development. Finally, if you meet the requirements, you have a chance at becoming a partner somewhat more quickly in a large firm than in a small firm.

So much for the advantages of spending your first few years in accounting with a large public firm. There are some disadvantages as well. For example, in a larger firm you run the risk of being pigeonholed a little too early in your career. You could find yourself spending all your time in one industry or with one client. One accountant I know spent three years working on one audit for one airline. Mind you, this might have been an excellent job for this accountant, but usually accountants who become too narrowly specialized early in their careers are jeopardizing their chances for advancement later on. I know one accountant, for instance, who spent a good deal of time in his early years working on consolidations. He became a specialist in consolidations, but within a few years grew tired of the work. It took him quite a while to reroute his career.

You should bear in mind, too, that the pressure to get ahead is more intense in the larger firms than it is in the medium-sized and smaller firms. Sometimes this pressure can get in the way of your development as an accountant. It's been my observation that the accountants who get ahead in the larger public accounting firms are slightly more politically aggressive than average, and they make it a point to "play the game." I don't say this disparagingly. I do think, though, that if you have ambitions to rise in the largest CPA firms, you can't sit back and wait to be noticed. You have to assert yourself early.

Many of the larger CPA firms are actually a conglomeration of small firms, with each partner having his or her own sphere of influence and with people permanently assigned to each partner. There is nothing wrong with this arrangement, but you should realize that if you are working with such a firm, you are not so much working with the *firm* as you are for one or several people. That puts your rise or fall in their hands. For better or for worse, they are your mentors.

The smaller and medium-sized firms do not lend themselves to the kinds of generalizations that apply to the larger firms. They vary enormously in terms of the kind of training you'll get, the kind of work you'll do, and the conditions under which you'll work. Some firms put junior staff members in charge of small audits within a few months. Other firms are more conservative. In some firms, you'll feel the pressure to bring in new business, but usually this won't be the case.

Overall, the main advantage of working for a relatively small firm—if the firm is a good one—is that you can learn more in a shorter period of time than you can in a larger firm. Buddy Martin, CPA, attributes his success today to the fact that he was able to spend his first three years in accounting with a small firm in which the senior partners were constantly out in the field with him. "It wasn't just accounting I learned," he says. "It was how to deal with clients and with special situations. Unfortunately, there are not that many firms today that can give a young accountant this kind of experience."

To sum up, the *size* of the firm you join when you take your first job in accounting is not nearly as important as the *quality* of the firm and the relevance of the experience you're likely to have to your long-term career goals. Make the choice carefully, for it could have far more bearing on your career success than you might imagine.

PUBLIC VERSUS MANAGEMENT ACCOUNTING

Clearly, one of the fundamental decisions an accountant who intends to stay in accounting and doesn't want to start a private practice must make is whether to establish a career path in public or management accounting. (There are other career paths, such as in government; but the vast majority of accountants are in either public accounting or management accounting.)

Before getting into the differences, let me make this overall observation: I know as many successful and satisfied accountants in public accounting as in management accounting. I also know dissatisfied and relatively unsuccessful accountants in both public and management accounting. In other words, neither public accounting nor management accounting has a monopoly on opportunity or job satisfaction. In the end, it's your decision as to which you are better suited for.

The Nature of the Work

During World War II, Eli Mason, CPA, spent 2 years as a controller in a defense plant in New York City, and Harry Gilbert, CPA, found himself a finance officer in the army. For both men, it was their first taste of private accounting.

When the war ended, Mason went back to public accounting and established the firm of Mason & Company. Says Mason, "I found public accounting more challenging than being in the same place every day and dealing with the same problems." Gilbert, however, decided to stay in private accounting. Says Gilbert: "I had always loved public accounting, and before the war, I had no desire to leave it. Then, for the first time, I had a taste of what it was like not having to go from client to client, and for the first time I didn't have to suppress the frustration I sometimes used to feel when I was working with a client whose intelligence I didn't respect and yet who was earning 50 times what I was earning. In the army, I got a taste of what it was like to be a kingpin in an organization, and I liked it."

The question of which branch of accounting, public or private, is more interesting, enjoyable, and lucrative is an ongoing debate, and you're not going to find me taking any sides. As Eli Mason explains it, "In the end, it's all a matter of personality." It's possible, however, to make a few generalizations.

One of my observations over the years has been that public accounting is better suited to people who enjoy pure accounting per se, whereas management accounting is better suited for people who are interested more in business than they are in accounting. I've noticed, too, that private accountants, as a group, seem to prefer concentrating on one set of problems—those of the company they work for—and like to deal with the same people every day rather than service a number of different clients.

There are other differences. "Public accountants are probably a little more analytical as a rule than management accountants," says Frank Davidson. "They generally refer to the pieces once they've been put together, whereas management accountants are more interested in the day-to-day decisions that put the pieces together in the first place."

Adds Charles Wolff: "To succeed in public accounting you have to be the type who likes to sink your teeth into a project and develop it from an idea to completion."

A lot of it has to do, too, with how much you relish the pressure of the profession. There is pressure, of course, in both public and private accounting, but most people would agree that the pressure is greater in public accounting. The pressure has to do not only with the job itself— the deadlines come more frequently and you're under the gun from more sources—but also with the pressures that public accounting puts on your home life because of the travel and the long hours.

"If you're married, you need a very understanding spouse to succeed in public accounting," says Larry D. Gipple, CPA, the administrative personnel partner of McGladrey Hendrickson & Co. "We lose more good people because of marital relationships than we do from the pressure per se." Adds Don Prince, CPA, from our Pittsburgh franchise, "Some people simply can't handle the tremendous pressure and time demands of public accounting. You don't just work for a boss; you also work for a client who has unreasonable demands—some of them on weekends."

On the other hand, the pressures in management accounting are more a reflection of the company and the person you work for than the job. At their worst, the pressures you're up against in private accounting are not nearly as great as those in most public firms.

Where the Money Is

It used to be said that you could earn more money in private accounting than you could in public accounting. This may still be true at the middle levels of each, but at the entry levels, according to the *Prevailing Financial and Data Processing Starting Salaries* guide published each year by Robert Half International, Inc., accountants in large and medium-sized public firms earn, on the average, about 16 percent *more* than internal accountants working in private industry. At the upper levels, it's safe to assume, there really isn't much difference at all. The earnings of the managing partners of the largest public accounting firms are on a par with those of *Fortune* 500 CEO salaries. I also know partners in medium-sized CPA firms who, because of the deals they've had access to, have made far more money than they could have hoped to have earned in private industry; by most standards, these partners are considered quite wealthy.

If there are differences in the earning capacities of accounting positions, the factor appears to be the size of the company or firm, rather than whether you're in public or private accounting. The average corporate controller starting with a company whose yearly volume is between $10 million and $50 million was making between $37,000 and $50,000 in 1983. Controllers working for companies with volume in excess of $750 million, on the other hand, were earning between $95,000 and $135,000. Similar differences, though not quite as dramatic, prevail in public accounting as well.

Where there is definitely a difference between public and private accounting is in job security, for there is no question but that public accounting offers more security than private accounting. "Public accountants who are good technicians have what amounts to almost guaranteed employment," maintains Frank Bartl, CPA, who is associated with our Long Island franchise. "Public accountants can change jobs at any time because they have a trade, and there's a market out there for them as long as they can function."

The same is not true in private accounting. First of all, it is much easier for a public accountant to move into private accounting than it is for a private accountant to move into public accounting. Public firms, except in rare situations, would almost always prefer to hire someone with a career background in public accounting. Second, experience in private accounting is not as easily transferable from one job to another. If you're a management accountant with many years of experience in, say, food service companies, you're going to have trouble convincing an oil company that you are qualified for a job in that company. Third, because private accountants don't have the contacts the public accountants develop, their job possibilities are more limited than those of public accountants. "Private accountants," says Buddy Martin, "don't have as wide a world to choose from as public accountants do."

Making the Move from Public to Private Accounting

Years ago, I knew a CPA—let's call him Jack—who had been associated with a major public accounting firm for more than 15 years. One day he asked me to lunch. "Bob," he told me, "I have to get out of this company. I don't like most of the people here, and they don't like me. I'm never going to make partner. What I'd really like is to get out of public accounting and become a controller in a good company."

On the surface, Jack's ambition to leave public accounting and get into management seemed reasonable enough. Thousands of public accountants make the same kind of move every year. Only one thing was wrong. When you've been in public accounting for as long as Jack had been—15 years—it is tough to land a good job in private accounting—unless, that is, you can connect with a client firm. I could have gotten Jack a job, but it would have been with a relatively small company and he would have had to take a salary cut.

As it happens, I convinced Jack to stay put, and eventually he became a partner in the firm, but he is no exception. I have met many accountants like him: accountants who have wanted to move from public to private accounting but simply waited too long to make the move. The reason I say "too late" is that the most sought-after positions in accounting—partnerships in the public firms and CFO positions in industry—are not positions you can wake up one day and decide you want. You have to plan years in advance for them.

Granted, there are exceptions. Donald H. Trautlein, chairman of Bethlehem Steel, spent 25 years at Price Waterhouse before he joined Bethlehem. However, as is almost always the case when the move to private accounting takes place after so long a period of time, Trautlein was already handling the account (Bethlehem) at Price Waterhouse. More typically, the accountants who have gone the furthest in industry have made the shift from public to private accounting fairly early in their careers. Harold S. Geneen, CPA, chairman of International Telephone and Telegraph, left Lybrand, Ross Bros. & Montgomery (now Coopers & Lybrand) to become chief accountant for an American Can Company subsidiary in 1942, about 7 years after he joined Lybrand. James L. Ketelsen, CPA, president and chief executive officer of Tenneco Inc., spent 4 years in public accounting before joining a Tenneco subsidiary as an assistant controller. J. Paul Lyet, CPA, chairman and chief executive officer of the Sperry Rand Corporation, spent only 2 years with Ernst & Ernst before joining the Sperry New Holland farm equipment division as controller.

Most successful accountants I've spoken to advise young accountants who want to move into corporate finance at the Fortune 500 level to spend at least 3 or 4 years with a good CPA firm. By "good" they're not necessarily talking about a large firm, but about a firm that has more than a few major clients. I would add that if you are contemplating a career in private accounting, you do not stay in public accounting for more than 6 or 7 years.

Another point worth stressing here is that when you *do* make the move, choose the company with care. It's understandable, once you've been with a good public accounting firm for 4 or 5 years, to want a position with stature and responsibility, such as a controllership, and frequently there may be a controllership available, albeit in a very small firm with no great future.

Keep in mind that successful companies will rarely put you into a controllership position directly from public accounting—unless you've already been involved with that company for many years. So when you make your move, you have to think 3 or 4 years down the road, rather than dead-end yourself in a position that has no future. Don't hesitate to start with a good corporation as an internal auditor if the advancement opportunities are reasonably clear. You'll be able to get a good perspective of the entire operation, meet the right executives throughout the company, and subtly influence getting an attractive job transfer.

CAREER PATHING: OTHER CONSIDERATIONS

Even if you've chosen (or been chosen by) a firm that fits well into your career plan, you still have a number of decisions to make that will go a long way in determining your ultimate career success. Here are some of the considerations and what you should bear in mind about each.

THE CPA CERTIFICATE

I know of many accountants who have never become CPAs and have nonetheless done very well in accounting. Then again, these accountants represent a vanishing minority. The CPA certificate has always been a useful career asset but, as our Burke study showed, virtually 100 percent of the CPA partners and chief financial officers queried considered being a CPA "important"—and the CPA certificate is becoming increasingly important each year.

It isn't only that being a CPA automatically increases your earning power (in private accounting, for instance, CPAs earn an average of 10 percent more than non-CPAs), it's more that not being a CPA limits your career options. If you're not certified, you can almost forget about becoming a partner in a CPA firm. (You can, however, become successful as a non-CPA in a CPA firm by being a recognized expert in a specialty or by being an effective business getter.)

It's possible, of course, that you have no intention of staying in accounting, in which case you might consider sitting for the CPA exam a waste of your time. I don't agree. I still have the CPA credential, even though I've been out of accounting for more than 35 years. Being a CPA gave me a recognizable career credential.

THE CMA

As yet, the certificate in management accounting has neither the prestige nor the numbers that the CPA license can claim. (There are a few more than 3100 CMAs today as compared with more than 200,000 CPAs.) Even so, I think the CMA is an important credential that will become increasingly important in years to come, and therefore well worth pursuing. In Canada and England, for instance, an accountant who holds the equivalent of the U.S. CMA has almost as much recognition as the accountant who is a chartered accountant (CA). Chartered accountants and industrial accountants are not licensed, but their associations are very strong, and if, for some reason, an accountant is dismissed from the association, his or her career could be severely damaged.

My personal view of the CMA situation is that it should be tied into the licensing of management accountants. Management accountants, like CPAs, should have to be approved and certified by a state board, and passing the CMA exam should be a requirement. (However, all CPAs and those practicing as management accountants should be grand-fathered.) I'm well aware that many CPA partners do not share my viewpoint and see no reason for licensing management accountants, but more and more CPAs are at least beginning to appreciate that management accountants need more official recognition from the accounting profession.

Norman Auerbach, for instance, feels that to be "a totally professional" person, an accountant should have a strong educational base—at least 5 years of classes. At the conclusion of the period of study, the person could qualify as a professional accountant by passing an examination. "Thereafter," he says, "if an accountant wants to go into management and industry, he or she should work for 2 years and then take the CMA exam. If this accountant wants to go into public accounting after 2 years of CPA experience, he or she would take the CPA exam. This would offer greater professional stature to accountants, irrespective of their area of interest."

Interestingly enough, the CMA exam may be more difficult in some ways than the CPA exam because it covers a broader range of areas, among them economics, statistics, banking, and finance. Thus, passing the exam indicates to prospective employers that you have achieved a certain level of expertise. Also, as Dr. James Bulloch, managing director of the Institute of Management Accounting, points out, "Passing the CMA demonstrates to other people your commitment to further personal and business development, and you show that your interest goes beyond the narrow confines of the job you're now working in."

According to surveys taken by the Institute of Management Accounting, accountants who have become CMAs have nothing but praise for the program. Of the more than 3100 accountants who have passed the examination, 97 percent would recommend the CMA program to other accountants. Apart from their feeling that the CMA has helped advance their careers, many cited the personal challenge and feeling of satisfaction that came from passing the exam.

How important will the CMA be over the next 10 years? It's difficult to say. James Bulloch estimates that in time, as the National Association of Accountants, through its Institute of Management Accounting, continues to promote the CMA, there will be some 30,000 CMAs. And Edward Lutz, who has as broad a perspective of accounting as anyone, says flatly that if he had a son or daughter who was interested in accounting, he would recommend sitting for both the CPA and the CMA examinations. My own feeling about the CMA, which I've expressed in many articles, is that it's an achievement and a credential that's well worth a management accountant's time.

HOW MUCH SHOULD YOU SPECIALIZE?

Becoming knowledgeable in one particular specialty—taxation, for instance—can undoubtedly be useful as a career strategy. Specialists often earn more money than nonspecialists, and the reason many clients switch auditors, according to changes listed in the *Public Accounting Report,* is to get the services of a firm that specializes in their particular industry or discipline.

But if specialization can earn you a slightly higher salary and can benefit the firm you work for, it doesn't necessarily benefit you in the long run. It may actually serve to limit your career options, for your appeal is limited to firms that have a need for your specialty. Yes, if you're a top specialist, it's possible to earn more than some of the partners in the firm, but what is in vogue today may not be in vogue tomorrow. Who would have guessed in the mid-1970s, for instance, that accountants who specialized in the oil and gas industry would not be in great demand in the early 1980s?

HOW IMPORTANT IS THE MBA?

It's clear that more and more young accountants are getting their MBAs. Our Burke survey suggests that an MBA is more important in management accounting than in public accounting. Some 82 percent of top management personnel and 72 percent of chief financial officers felt that an accountant with an MBA was more likely to get ahead. Only 59 percent of CPA partners felt the same way. More significantly, roughly one out of four CPA partners queried took issue with the idea that an MBA was helpful to an accountant's career, whereas only 8 percent of top corporate management and 15 percent of chief financial officers saw little value in the MBA.

"I don't think an MBA is *vital,*" says Peter Skomorowsky, CPA, who heads the New York office of Alexander Grant, "but it gave me a broader base of ideas than I think I would otherwise have had. I think the viewpoint instilled by the MBA program is valuable, but I'm not convinced you need to be an MBA to *have* that viewpoint."

As I see it, timing has a lot to do with the relative value of the MBA. If you can afford to get your MBA before you start to work full time, go ahead and do it. However, given a choice between concentrating full time on your first accounting job or dividing your time between work and graduate studies, you are better off devoting your energy to the job.

I am not minimizing the importance of the MBA, either as a learning experience or a credential, but what will ultimately determine your success is job performance and not degrees.

CAREER PATHING: SOME FINAL CONSIDERATIONS

Career pathing is probably the most difficult aspect of the accounting profession on which to offer specific advice. It's difficult, for one thing, to know what your ultimate goals are, and once you establish these goals, it's no mean trick to chart and to follow the path most likely to reach these goals.

If there is a key to successful career planning, it's being willing to take the time, periodically throughout your career, to reexamine your situation carefully. You continually have to ask yourself if the career goals you formulated 2 or 3 years ago are as important to you today. You have to take a hard look to determine whether you are closer today to those goals than you were when you first formulated them. You also have to be alert to any new situations that may have arisen in your job or in your firm that could have an impact on your career goals. Perhaps your career is moving in a direction that is inconsistent with what you eventually want out of accounting. Perhaps, out of necessity, you've been thrust into a role that may be benefiting the firm but is not taking you in the direction in which you want to go.

Above all, you need to be flexible. One of the more interesting career paths I uncovered in my interviews was that of Dennis A. Osterdock, a CPA who now runs his own consulting firm in Fairbanks, Alaska. Osterdock's original career goal was to join his father's CPA firm in Stockton, California, and so he spent his first 2 years out of college with Price Waterhouse, planning all along to join his father's firm within a few years. "Then I decided," he said, "to spend a year looking around before I finally settled in with my father."

During that year Osterdock applied for—and got—a job with a small land development company in Fairbanks and a year later he found himself a part owner of Alaska Airlines. Not too long afterward, Osterdock decided to go back to Stockton and work with his father, but, as he puts it, "My heart was really in Alaska." He returned to Alaska, set up a management consulting firm, and eventually went into partnership with another man in a steel fabricating company. "We ran the company together for two years," Osterdock explains, "and then we brought in an employee from Seattle to run things. That's when I started looking around for something else to do and decided that Alaska needed a good recruiting firm."

Osterdock can't say for sure what he'll be doing 5 years from today, but he's convinced that his willingness to move in directions he didn't originally think of has not only helped to make him successful but has given him a rich and fulfilling background. His is not the classic career path, but it's not a bad one to keep in mind.

CHAPTER FIVE **HOW TO HANDLE YOURSELF ON THE JOB**

There's no such thing as not having enough time if you're doing what you want to do.

As I've been stressing all along in this book, career success in accounting depends upon qualities that go beyond technical expertise, and the further you advance in the profession, the more important these qualities become. What, exactly, *are* these other qualities—the qualities that, when combined with technical competence, differentiate successful accountants from the accountants struggling to hold their own in the middle levels?

I put this question to nearly everyone I interviewed for this book and, as you might expect, I received a variety of answers. Eli Mason, for instance, talked in terms of feeling a sense of responsibility "to your clients, to your profession, and to the public." William Kanaga talked about learning how to view problems through the eyes of the client. Bob Anderson stressed motivation, noting that almost all the accountants he has observed who have failed to achieve career potential were insufficiently motivated. William S. Wernersback, a partner in Pannell Kerr Forster, emphasized dedication and the ability to communicate: "We look for people," he says, "who can dedicate themselves and who can communicate not only with clients but within the organization as well."

Saul Silverman talked about a combination of qualities. "You need competence, compassion, and understanding," he said, "but at the same time you need a level of professional independence." Dr. Emanuel Saxe, a CPA and prominent educator, stressed, among other things, the importance of being able to think logically. "Since auditing involves the making of many important judgments," he said, "it is most important that they be based upon sound reasoning."

I was especially intrigued by the observation of Dr. Abraham J. Briloff, CPA, author of *Unaccountable Accounting, More Debits Than Credits* and *The Truth About Corporate Accounting*. Briloff talks of the qualities that distinguish accountants as a "series of interrelated I's." He talks first of "intellectual competence" and adds "independence." "The third," he says, "would be integrity, which dovetails with independence." Briloff mentions the quality of intrepidity, which he defines as the "ability or the willingness to take risks for what one considers to be desirable rather than just determining to go along because that's the way you might get along." He also talks about "pensive indignation," which means "the willingness to speak out overtly when we see wrong prevailing." Finally, in Briloff's "series of I's," there is what he calls the ultimate I—which is how each individual relates to the totality of relationships.

I can do little more than echo the views expressed by the accountants I've just mentioned. Motivation, dedication to the profession, clear thinking, a sense of responsibility to the people you work with or for, integrity, good judgment—these and others are crucial qualities for accountants seeking success. But *having* these qualities is not enough. You have to be able to demonstrate these qualities day after day on your job. In this chapter, we'll look at the various ways you can do this.

BE A TEAM PLAYER

I don't know of any accounting firm or any corporation (of any size) that doesn't put a high premium on company loyalty. "It's a very positive attribute," says William Morgan of Peat Marwick Mitchell. "The fact that you're proud of your organization can't help but show itself in everything you do, particularly in your dealings with clients."

You demonstrate company loyalty in any number of different ways. The easiest—and the most important—way is to support your company policies. But there are other, subtler things that can demonstrate loyalty and pride: little things that you might not think about, like being punctual and putting in a *full* day's work; being willing, when the need arises, to work extra hours; and being pleasant and courteous to all the people you work with, from the receptionist to the head of the firm.

These are little things, but don't underestimate their importance. Many times these qualities alone—punctuality, caring, the willingness to work hard—have induced companies to keep, and eventually promote, people they might otherwise have terminated. I can recall one situation in particular in which a not especially good accountant in a Wall Street firm was promoted to customer service because the company didn't want to fire an employee who was loyal and hardworking.

One of the most difficult things about being a team player, not only in accounting but in any job, is getting along with a boss who may not be the easiest person to deal with. Many accountants who want to make a change are looking for this very reason: They don't get along with their supervisors. But I've noticed that many accountants who leave jobs because they don't get along with their boss run into the same problems in their new jobs. On the other hand, when I asked one of the most successful accountants I ever met to explain his rapid rise in one of the large CPA firms, he said to me, "I always made my boss look good."

It is part of your job responsibility not only to get along with your supervisors but to make their lives easier. One way to do this is to make up your mind to do more than follow orders. In other words, do your best to *anticipate* your boss's needs. You should know, for instance, the communication style your boss prefers: whether he or she likes you to spell things out in detail or simply give the rough outline of a project. You should be able to sense when your boss is under pressure and pitch in to ease the pressure. You should also know as much as you can about the person your boss reports to and the kinds of pressure this person puts on your boss. The better you can understand these stresses, the better you'll be able to anticipate them. I repeat: Whatever you can do to make your boss's life easier and to make your boss look better will generally enhance your own career progress.

The last aspect of being a team player is giving your company your full time and your best effort. This isn't always easy, particularly if you're pursuing an advanced degree at night, which is why I advise young accountants who are just beginning with a firm to think twice before jumping into graduate school. As I mentioned earlier, advanced degrees do give you an edge in the marketplace, but if in the course of pursuing the degree, you reduce your contribution to your company during the day, I think you're making a mistake. "The big problem," says Alex Cohen, publisher of *The Practical Accountant*, "is simple energy. I don't care who you are. If you're going to school 2 or 3 nights a week, you simply can't give your firm the extra time when necessary. You lack flexibility."

MOONLIGHTING: YES OR NO?

The same principle applies to moonlighting. For many, the temptation to pick up extra money on the side doing tax work, write-ups, and consulting is understandable, but many public accounting firms prohibit their employees from moonlighting as accountants and frown on moonlighting in general.

This prohibition apart, the vast majority of the accountants I've seen who moonlight do not move as far in their companies as accountants who give their full-time effort to their primary job. I believe in putting all my eggs in one basket and then watching that basket.

If you decide to moonlight, two words of caution. First, don't keep it from your company, and second, do not under any circumstances link the name of your employer in your private practice. A CPA firm I worked for years ago fired a manager at the peak of the tax season because they found he was doing his own tax work on the side and, worse, was trading on his company's name with his after-hours clients.

Obviously, giving all your attention to the job you currently hold doesn't always pay big dividends, but that's the risk you accept when you join an organization. My feeling has always been that many accountants never really dig in and give their job everything they can. I'm not talking about sacrificing every other part of your life for your job—not at all. I'm talking about giving the job everything it's worth—and a little more.

SEE THE TOTALITY OF YOUR JOB

One of the themes that recurred again and again in the conversations I have had with accountants is the importance of seeing past the numbers and, in particular, of being able to relate these numbers to the overall business objectives. "The further you go in accounting," says Pat Southerland, from the District of Columbia, "the more important your ability to look beyond the numbers you're working on becomes. If you're doing the accounts receivable section of an audit, the question you have to ask yourself is how all of this interacts with other sections. If you run into a problem, you have to see how that problem relates not only to you, but to everybody else."

Too many accountants are unable to do what Southerland talks about. They manifest what Buddy Martin calls "tunnel vision." "They don't see the whole picture from the client's point of view," says Martin. "They see only a set of numbers, and they don't relate to the people those numbers represent."

The only way to gain the correct perspective is to broaden your business and intellectual horizons in any way you can. You should be educating yourself (assuming the courses and seminars you take don't interfere with your daily responsibilities) above and beyond the requirements of the Continuing Professional Education (CPE) and beyond the requirements of the AICPA and of many states and the SEC.

If you're in public accounting, you should make it your business to learn as much as you can about each client you work with: not just how much money it earns, but the history of the company, the products it sells, and the people who run the company. And as a management accountant, you should be thoroughly familiar not only with your own company, but with the industry of which it's a part. What's more, even though the continuing education requirements aren't as formalized as they are in public accounting, you should still continue to educate yourself in the state of the art.

One of the best ways, apart from going to school and reading, to gain broad knowledge is to seek out someone who has been with the company a long time and to get as much information from this person as you can. In other words, find a good mentor. "Too many young accountants," says Saul Silverman, "fail to realize what a valuable resource they have in the older members of the firm they work for. Most people who've been with a company for a long time are flattered when a younger accountant comes to them for help and information. I know that in my career when younger people have come to me for information or advice, I was only too pleased to give it, and I was always surprised when there were employees who tried to do it all alone."

KNOW WHERE THE POWER IS

I've never seen a company (or any organization, for that matter), that wasn't "political" to some degree—political in the sense that certain people in the organization hold power disproportionate to their position. All things considered, accounting is probably a little *less* political than other areas of business, but to say that as an accountant you don't have to concern yourself with company politics would be naive.

In some cases, you may find that getting ahead in your firm will be tied to your ability to emulate the style of top management. I worked for a firm once in which one of my coworkers emulated almost everything about the president of the company, from the way he walked, to facial expressions—even to the kind of cigars the boss smoked. Not surprisingly, my coworker became the president's "fair-haired boy." (Then again, when the company was sold, guess who was one of the first to be let go?)

One of the best, if not one of the easiest, ways of gaining recognition is to take on those jobs that no one else wants to do—providing, that is, that you're doing them for the right person and providing it's the right kind of job. Taking on a boring assignment—a one-day trip to an out-of-town bank to examine one stock certificate—is likely to be unappreciated. But taking charge of the United Way campaign in your firm, while it might seem a thankless job, could gain you important recognition, especially if the chairperson of the campaign is somebody with power.

Yet another way to gain recognition is to anticipate your firm's needs, which you can do by analyzing where your firm's weaknesses may lie and by making it your business to develop strengths in these areas. Dan Kramer recalls that in the early years of Oppenheim Appel Dixon & Co., his ability to write gave him a special niche with partners and managers. "It got to the point," he said, "where almost any correspondence that went out of the firm had to go through me first. I saw everything that went out, and people would come to me and want to know, 'When did we do this or that?' I was one of the few people they could come to because I had hands-on exposure to a great deal of the accounting firm's information."

Just imagine, for example, if years ago you could have foreseen the role of computers in accounting and you had learned about computers before anybody else in the organization knew anything about them. You wouldn't necessarily have to know how to program the computer. Simply knowing what's around and what's suitable for your company might have been enough to give you additional stature.

LEARN HOW TO MANAGE YOUR TIME

Time is in short supply for accountants, and few skills you develop in your professional career will have more bearing on your progress than your ability to manage your time efficiently.

Most good accountants are detail oriented. But sometimes this concern for detail can get out of hand. You can spend so much time trying to resolve a 35-cent discrepancy that you overlook a $1 million error. A CPA friend of mine was complaining recently to me about an accountant who, if he is testing a month of bills for an audit and can't find a particular invoice, immediately decides to check another 100 invoices. "What I'd like my auditors to do," the CPA says, "is to use some judgment. You have to ask yourself in a situation like this if the lost invoice is an isolated instance or indicates a possible lack of control because of a poor filing or a poor control system. The point is to take a few minutes to look at the forest rather than wasting an hour concentrating on one tree."

Most successful accountants have their individual system of managing their time. "What I try to do," says Peat Marwick Mitchell's William Morgan, "is to implement some basic time management techniques, as opposed to trying to do everything at once. I look each day at what has to be done, and what's come in, and what should be handled in terms of client affairs. Then I try to prioritize those things and put together a realistic list of what can get accomplished that day."

I shouldn't have to remind you to begin each of your work days with a written agenda. The agenda should list all the tasks that you need to attend to that day, each ranked according to its priority. Not all of these tasks are going to be equally appealing, but try to resist the temptation of postponing the unpleasant ones. "In my experience," says William S. Kanaga, chairman of Arthur Young & Company, "when you put off dealing with a problem, the problem only gets worse. So I make it a point, if there is a really tough problem on my desk, to deal with it immediately. Dealing with the problem may not be something I enjoy doing, but by dealing with it, I'm able to operate more effectively."

Apart from planning your day in advance, you have to make sure that you've allotted enough time to handle each of the tasks you've set down on your agenda. If it looks as if there is too much work for you to handle, don't be afraid to admit that you can't handle the workload. Successful people, as a rule, are not embarrassed to speak up and to ask for help if they're overloaded. They're not afraid that by admitting they have too much work they're showing a weakness. Follow their example.

Finally, if you haven't already done so, I strongly recommend that you maintain a time log for at least 1 week. Don't make it complicated. Simply keep a legal pad or a daily appointment sheet near your desk and record on it what you are working on and how long it's taking to do each phase of the task.

Once you've completed a time log for at least 5 days, you're ready to evaluate how efficiently you're managing your time. Record on a separate sheet of paper all the tasks you've been involved with that week and how much total time throughout the week you spent on each. Then figure out the total amount of hours you worked that week. Now you're ready to analyze whether you're spending the bulk of your time on the most important facets of your job.

ASKING FOR A RAISE

When it comes to asking for a raise, most accountants are no different from business professionals in general. They aren't especially comfortable with the idea of asking their companies for more money (regardless of how justified they may be in their request), and once they decide they're going to ask for the raise, they don't really know how to go about it.

There are any number of reasons asking for a raise is so difficult an undertaking for so many people, not the least of which is the difficulty many people have in placing a value on their services. But rather than dwell on these reasons, let's look briefly at some of the points to keep in mind when you decide to seek a raise.

1. *Prepare a strong case*: Before going into any salary discussion, make sure you've prepared a case that argues strongly for your raise request. The case should be built around your *accomplishments* in the company and not your personal financial needs.
2. *Know what you're worth*: Knowing how much the competition—and your own company—pays accountants with experience, ability, and seniority similar to yours should give you a rough idea of how much you're worth to your company and serve as the basis of your negotiations.
3. *Know when to ask*: The best time to seek a salary increase (periodic salary reviews notwithstanding) is shortly after you've successfully completed an important project that has benefited the company. The worst time to seek a salary increase, on the other hand, is when the company is going through a difficult time.
4. *Be flexible*: You should always go into a salary discussion with two figures in mind: (1) what you'd like and (2) what you'll settle for. Regardless of how justified you feel your request to be, never hand down an ultimatum.

HANDLING STRESS

Stress is inherent in most occupations, and accounting is certainly no exception. Nearly everything accountants do embodies a deadline of one kind or another: from a corporate client, from the government, from a supervisor. "And it's not so much the deadline itself," says Robert McCall, a CPA who owns our New Orleans office. "It's the fact that most people who are not accountants themselves simply cannot understand the kind of deadline pressure you're under. They're looking for figures, but what they don't realize is the sequence you need to go through in order to get the figures."

Some of the stress that is so much a part of accounting is, of course, necessary. "If we never felt stress in our day-to-day responsibilities," says William Kanaga, "it would mean that we were unaffected by the problems of our clients and that we'd probably lose them. It would mean that we didn't have a real and abiding interest in their problems." I think it's true, too, as Kanaga observes, that there is a weeding out process of a sort in public accounting. The accountants who can't deal with the pressure tend to leave public accounting relatively early in their careers.

Granting that stress, in small degrees, can make you a better accountant and granting, too, that most accountants who don't deal well with stress usually end up in less stressful positions, stress remains a major problem in accounting—so much so that the AICPA has begun to offer seminars that address the problem as it applies not only to individual accountants but also to their spouses.

Few people, I think, appreciate and understand the extent of the problem of stress in accounting more than Ken Macjen (pronounced MA-son), who directs the personnel assistance program for Ernst & Whinney. This program, which was started in 1977, is designed to help the firm's accountants work through some of the stress-related problems that public accounting can often produce. "I had some personal problems of my own that had to do with stress," says Macjen. "And once I was able to solve them, with a lot of help from others, I decided I wanted to do what I could to help other people."

Macjen spends the bulk of his time counseling both accountants and their spouses. The reason he spends so much time with spouses, he explains, is that of all the stress-related problems that could affect accountants—such as alcohol, drugs, and personal relationships—the most common are marital problems.

"The problems are the most severe," Macjen says, "in those situations in which their spouses are unable to accept how difficult it is for CPAs in public accounting to meet the demands of their firm, their clients, and their families, not to mention the demands they make on themselves." He adds: "The best marriages that include a CPA are those in which the spouses understand and accept that they may not *always* come first and also recognize that it's the quality, not the quantity, of the time that's important."

While conceding that some marital problems are difficult to avoid, Macjen maintains that many accountants compound their marital problems by putting added pressure on themselves. "What it comes down to in many marriages," he says, "is that many accountants are unable to separate what they do at the office from what they do at home."

To illustrate his point, Macjen tells of a woman he once spoke to at one of the meetings he holds periodically with the spouses of CPAs. Her CPA husband, according to the woman, traveled frequently, and whenever he would leave for a trip at the beginning of a week, he would give his wife a yellow pad that had a "do" list on it. The pad listed a beginning cash balance. The wife was expected during the week not only to complete all the "do's" but also to keep a running balance of all expenditures. "The first thing my husband always does when he comes home at the end of the week," she said, "is to check off the 'do' list, and then make sure that the balance is correct. I get even with him, though. I'll lose a receipt on purpose, and this drives him out of his mind."

Macjen admits that this accountant's behavior is extreme, but he says that the syndrome typified by this person is by no means a rarity among accountants. "It's what psychologists call the 'perfectionist' syndrome," he says. "Accountants are not the only professionals affected by it, but it's more common in accounting than most people think."

The most frequent symptom of this syndrome, according to Macjen, is the inability to leave the job behind at the office. "Many accountants are so concerned with doing a good job," he says, "that they neglect every other aspect of their lives. When they're home, they're sitting in the den, talking to clients on the phone. They'll go on vacation, but they'll take work with them."

The problem with this approach to work, says Macjen, is that it is usually self-perpetuating. "What happens," he says, "is that problems occur at home, and the accountants, because they don't know how to deal with them, will throw themselves into their work all the more. Many become workaholics."

Ken Macjen feels that the only way many accountants can avoid this perfectionist syndrome is not to become so tied up in their careers that being a CPA is their only identity. "It isn't easy," he admits. "Many accountants have a tendency to internalize everything. They don't confront. And, too often, they're simply not willing to recognize that by pouring every bit of their energy into their jobs, they're really running away from personal problems."

It's to Ernst & Whinney's credit that they have a man like Ken Macjen doing personnel assistance work. More and more firms have begun to recognize that stress, when it gets out of hand, benefits no one. The result, in many cases, is the phenomenon referred to as "burnout."

You've heard the phrase, I'm sure. It was apparently coined by Dr. Herbert J. Freudenberger, of New York, whose early studies found a correlation between burnout and certain physiological symptoms, such as constant headaches and the inability to shake colds.

"Burnout occurs," says Dr. Harry Levinson, an industrial psychologist who has specialized in this area of stress, "when a person is unable to continue what he or she is doing. People who've burned out have to throw in the sponge. They've lost energy and commitment. They've shot their wad on a particular task."

I can tell you both from observation and from conversations I've had with hundreds of accountants that burnout is not at all uncommon in accounting. Says Marc Silbert, who heads our New York franchise, "The curious thing is that the accountants who are potential candidates for burnout are often excellent job candidates. Burnout is more common among overachievers than among people who coast."

The worst thing about burnout, according to psychologists who have studied the condition, is that you can be a victim without being aware of it until the condition is well advanced. That's why specialists like Dr. Levinson insist that probably the only way to combat burnout is to be sensitive to its early symptoms—symptoms that are frequently dismissed as temporary. Here are the symptoms:

- A feeling that no matter how hard you're working, you're not getting anywhere
- Apathy toward non-business-related tasks you once enjoyed (such as golf, tennis, music, getting together with friends)
- Chronic fatigue
- Irritability
- A sense of being besieged

Mind you, it is not at all unusual for accountants to experience some of these symptoms on occasion, particularly during very busy periods. But when these symptoms linger for weeks at a time, you should be concerned. When you find that your accounting work is the first thing you think about when you get up in the morning and the last thing you think about when you go to sleep at night, you're in trouble.

Bear in mind, too, that burnout is not a weakness. On the contrary. The accountants who are most susceptible to it are people who are highly energetic and have a great capacity for work. What do you do about it? Here are some suggestions from the experts:

- Recognize that burnout is a problem and that if you don't attend to it, it could seriously affect your health.

- If the problem is serious, schedule a reasonably lengthy vacation as soon as you can manage it.
- Regardless of how busy you are, do not schedule any work for the weekend and do what you can to limit the work you do at night.
- See what you can do about restructuring your work responsibilities. If you need help, don't be embarrassed to ask for it.
- Pace yourself differently throughout the day. Take frequent breaks, even if it's a 5-minute walk around the floor to break the tension.

HANDLING STRESS: SOME PRACTICAL ADVICE

Not surprisingly, most successful accountants have figured out a way to manage the stress in their day-to-day lives. The observations of Main Hurdman's William Aiken might be helpful to you. Aiken is convinced that the key to dealing with the stress of accounting is, first of all, being able to identify when you are in a situation that is more stressful than the norm. "With me," he says, "it's the fact that I'm perspiring more than usual. With other people, it might be that their heart is beating faster. But whatever the sign, I recognize it, and than I make every effort to remain as calm as I can."

When Aiken feels himself becoming unusually stressed, he takes a number of practical steps. Sometimes he will close the door and tell his secretary to hold all calls. "With the door open," he says, "the sense of a stressful environment intensifies. With the door closed, I feel a greater sense of tranquility." Another thing William Aiken does in times of stress is to find a different place to work. "I'll take what I'm working on," he says, "and go into a conference room. It's amazing what the change in environment can do to relax you."

Still another device that Aiken and other accountants I know rely on to minimize stress is to narrow the focus of their task. "I find that if I can clear my desk of everything except the project I'm working on," Aiken says, "I don't feel as flooded and I can think more clearly."

There are any number of other ways to minimize the effects of stress. For instance, I would urge you, even if you're extremely busy, not to have lunch brought into your office. Get away from the scene of the stress. Also, try to limit—and I know it's difficult—the amount of work you take home with you. Putting in 4 or 5 extra hours at home is understandable on occasion, but a steady diet of it can only wear you down in the long run.

This brings us, finally, to what may well be the most effective antidote to stress: your family and your coworkers. When Ken Macjen counsels accountants who are having problems, he emphasizes over and over the need to accept limitations and to shed the notion that asking for help is an admission of weakness. William Kanaga adds, "At Arthur Young none of the partners hesitates to ask for help when the need is there. You get brownie points for doing this."

KEEPING A PERSONNEL FILE

Whatever your specialty, you should be keeping your own personnel file. The file should contain a running record of every assignment, with the names and descriptions of the clients and the names of those with whom you had contact. The key point to bear in mind about this material is that it should highlight your accomplishments. Needless to say, the file should never include confidential or sensitive information.

Such a file will serve you well in several ways. To begin with, when the time comes for a salary review, you are in a position to present a strong case on your behalf—a case based on accomplishment. Second, such a file becomes invaluable should you decide to leave the firm. Your resumé will be much easier to put together and you'll have strong and complete facts to present to potential employers.

SOME FINAL THOUGHTS

As I mentioned early in this chapter, doing your job well is not enough to assure you of rapid progress through your firm. Equally important is making sure that management perceives you as a valuable member of the company. In this chapter we've covered some of the ways in which you can do this. Here is a summary of the points:

1. Show loyalty to the firm.
2. See the totality of your job.
3. Understand and anticipate your boss's needs.
4. Take credit (modestly) for your work.
5. Give coworkers and subordinates the same respect you give your supervisors.
6. Get recognition by taking on certain assignments nobody else will take.
7. Manage your time efficiently.
8. Be aware of—and take steps to counteract—job-related stress.

CHAPTER SIX **BECOMING A BETTER MANAGER**

The biggest failure of
management is the failure to
know what's going on.

It is no secret that management skills are not as highly developed in accounting as they are in many other occupations. The Burke study, for instance, found that 50 percent of top corporate management personnel and 37 percent of CPA partners felt that accountants are weak in managerial skills. These statistics are backed up by a study by Ralph L. Benke, a professor of accounting and director of the Center for Research in Accounting at James Madison University, Harrisonburg, Virginia.

Benke found that professionals don't leave CPA firms for more money, but for other reasons—chief of which is dissatisfaction with supervision. "Audit managers who leave," says Benke, "claim that partners are hard to please, don't praise good work, are not tactful, don't supervise enough, and are never around when they're needed." Interestingly, Benke found that the ability of the partners was rarely at issue. What was lacking, according to the terminating CPAs, was their ability to manage.

"There's no getting away from it." says Dr. Emanuel Saxe. "If you want to move to the top levels of the profession, and especially if you're looking to be a partner in one of the top firms, you have to be able to handle a large group of people intelligently and diplomatically. To be a partner, remember, you have to be chosen."

There can be no arguing the fact that if you can manage well and have a reasonable level of technical competence, you will go much further in most accounting job situations than you would if you had strong technical skills but were weak in management skills. When the partners of the major CPA firms are considering new partners, the qualities they now look for more than any other are the precise qualities that make for effective managing: the ability to get along well with people and the ability to *motivate* people. Observes Robert Palmer, CPA, publisher of the *Public Accounting Report*, "The most successful accountants I know are those who are technically competent but have been able to drop the characteristics of the technician and have been able to pick up the characteristics of a manager of people and a manager of events."

THE ESSENCE OF MANAGING

Probably the hardest thing for most accountants who move into a managerial position to accept is the fact they are now members of management and that their role goes beyond accumulating, recording, and auditing data. The manager's job is much more people oriented than before and calls for a new set of skills—skills most people do not come by naturally and most accountants have never mastered. Let's look into some of these management skills.

HIRING SMART

What holds true for baseball also holds true for accounting: Successful managing begins with surrounding yourself with the best possible talent—which is not necessarily the most expensive talent. From what I've observed, money usually isn't the main problem when it comes to hiring the right people. The problem is that too few people know how to pick and develop talent. Our Burke Marketing studies show that personnel departments rarely do the actual hiring. Except for lower salary-level jobs, you can expect, as a manager, to be doing your share of hiring. Therefore, it is important for you to sharpen your skills in picking the right people.

It's not easy to choose good people, and accountants are not the only professionals who have trouble when it comes to hiring the best people. Inefficient hiring practices are a universal problem in business today— so much so that among the most sought-after management training programs are those that teach interviewing techniques.

The Basics of Smart Hiring

Apart from the obvious—hiring the best people—two principles should govern your hiring practices. The first is always to hire with an eye toward your *total* staff and how they'll work together. In other words, having an entire staff of extremely talented people might not produce good results if the chemistry isn't right.

The second, and perhaps more important, principle is not to be afraid to hire someone better than yourself. Keep in mind that the better your staff members perform, the better you look. Your best people, far from endangering your job, will help you get ahead because you will be judged as someone who knows how to get the most out of your people. Let's look at some of the elements that will help you improve your skills at picking the right people.

How to Read a Resumé

If you're preparing to hire somebody, you are going to be reading dozens (maybe hundreds) of resumés, and you may use the resumés as a means of narrowing down the candidates you interview. Assuming you want to do the screening without professional assistance, there is nothing wrong with this practice. How else, after all, are you going to narrow down a long list of job candidates? What concerns me, though, is that a resumé is not necessarily a reflection of the accountant. I've seen some of the best resumés come from accountants I would have hesitated to recommend, and some mediocre resumés come from excellent candidates.

The fact is that the best resumés often come from job-jumpers, because they have the most experience writing resumés. The best way to get around this problem is to follow the example of astute clients of professional services, such as ours, who prefer to get their first look at the candidate and the resumé at the same time. In that way, the possibility of false impressions based on resumés is eliminated.

However, somewhere along the line you'll probably see the resumé, and it can still serve you well, providing you know what to look for. For instance, you should be wary of the following:

A functional resumé: A functional resumé is one that is not organized in the usual chronological form. Frequently this kind of resumé is used by an accountant who has a reason for not showing dates for employment. (He or she might be an excessive job-jumper.)

Excessive trivia: A resumé heavy with hobbies and interests usually denotes weakness in experience and skills.

A bitter tone: Signs of bitterness toward former employers can signal chronic discontent.

Sloppiness: A carelessly written resumé could indicate that it was prepared by an accountant with careless work habits.

So much for what you should be wary of. Here's what to look for:

Willingness to work hard: That trait is not easy to detect on a resumé, but you may be able to discern this quality by noting the accomplishments that went beyond the basics of the job.

Profit-mindedness and efficiency: Look for comments in the resumé in which the accountant mentions efficiency measures that helped increase earnings or helped improved the quality of the organization.

One other suggestion about reading a resumé: Start at the end. The reason is that most candidates put the least flattering information at the end of the resumé. By reading from the end forward, you may be able to save yourself some time.

Handling the Job Interview

It goes without saying that you should never hire anybody who will work directly with you unless you yourself conduct an interview. The problem, though, is that most accountants I've known are not particularly skilled at handling the job interview. If you use an applicant rating form like the one in Exhibit 1, you will be able to compare candidates more effectively.

"My advice to interviewers," says Philip Chenok, president of the AICPA, "is to look for the candidate's interest in the job. I was always concerned more with the questions candidates asked than I was with their answers to my question. I always tried to get a picture of the person's mind in action."

APPLICANT RATING

NAME _____ COLLEGE OR UNIVERSITY _____

ADDRESS _____

DATE INTERVIEWED _____ BY _____ OFFICE _____

PERSONAL GROOMING	Unkempt: Noticeable lack of neatness 1	No special care in dress or appearance 2	Neat and clean 3	Pays special attention to personal details 4	Immaculately dressed and groomed 5
PERSONAL MANNER	Nervous, embarrassed; compulsive mannerisms 1	Stiff, uncomfortable, ill at ease 2	No unusual tension, comfortable, at ease 3	Appears alert, free of tension 4	Unusually self-possessed and composed 5
EXPRESSION OF IDEAS	Unclear, illogical; speaks without thinking 1	Dwells on nonessentials; thoughts not well defined or expressed 2	Thoughts clearly expressed; words convey meaning 3	Convincing; thoughts developed logically 4	Unusual ability to express ideas logically 5
CONFIDENCE	Shy, retiring; arrogant, "cocky" 1	Submissive; argumentative 2	Reasonably self-assured, forthright 3	Shows self-confidence 4	Unusually self-assured; inspires confidence 5
MOTIVATION AND AMBITION	No drive, ambition limited 1	Little interest in development; seems satisfied 2	Interest and ambition fair; reasonable desire to work and develop 3	Definite future goals; wants to succeed and grow 4	Ambitions high, future well planned; evidence of personal development 5
EXPERIENCE AND EDUCATION	Education and experience unsuitable for the job 1	Education and experience not directly applicable 2	Good educational and work background; experience fair 3	Education and experience good; above average qualifications 4	Background especially well suited 5

Location Preference

_____

_____

_____

Rank in Class _____

Rank in Business School _____

Subjects of Most Interest, Other Than Accounting

Total _____

Military Obligation _____

Grade Point Average

Last Two Semesters

Accounting _____

Overall _____

Accounting _____

Overall _____

Overall Appraisal and Comments

_____

_____

_____

_____

REQUIRED THAT YOU CHECK ONE OF THE BOXES BELOW

Recommended and Classified by Me as —

A — ☐ Outstanding

B — ☐ Above Average

C — ☐ Average

D — ☐ Not Recommended

Signed _____

Date _____

500-12

Form 542.00(1)

EXHIBIT 1. Applicant Rating Form. (Reprinted with permission from Pannell Kerr Forster's *Personnel Management Policies and Procedures.*)

The questions a candidate asks do indeed give you a good glimpse into that candidate's mind, but you still have to control the interview. If there is any single key to gaining this control, it's your ability to get the most mileage out of each question you ask. Here are eight questions that are particularly good because they get candidates to reveal important characteristics without necessarily being aware of what they are making known:

1. *Why are you giving up your current job?* Be wary of accountants who bad-mouth their former employers. Remember, they could be malcontents and do the same thing to you a year or two down the road.

2. *What did you like best about your last job?* Candidates who can't give you a thoughtful answer to this question probably can't think beyond the mechanics of the job. They may lack depth.

3. *If you could have made improvements in your last job, what would you have done?* The answer to this question is a good reflection of creativity and sensitivity.

4. *Who was the most interesting client you had in your last job (or what was the most interesting job or project you've had so far in your career)?* The answer to this question will give you an idea of whether or not the candidate likes challenges and is perceptive.

5. *How would you describe the best person who ever worked for you or with you?* An accountant who has trouble answering this question could lack compassion.

6. *What kind of people annoy you the most?* Frequently, the traits mentioned by candidates *don't* apply to the candidates themselves.

7. *Can you describe some emergencies in some of your recent jobs in which you had to reschedule your time?* This is the question you ask instead of, "Are you willing to work extra hours when the situation calls for it?"

8. *In what way would you like our company to assist you if you join us?* Look for balance here. Be wary of accountants who indicate they may need a great deal of help and also of accountants who suggest that they may not want any help.

You can, of course, vary these questions in any number of ways, and not all of them may be appropriate for each interview. But I like them because the answers tell you a great deal about the candidate. Here is one additional word of advice: Try to be as relaxed and as conversational as possible when you ask these questions. In other words, don't conduct the interview as if it were an interrogation. Your objective is not to get the best of the candidate. It's to single out the one candidate who is best for the job.

Ending the Interview

Most job interviews drag on too long—past the point at which you have all the information you need to make a decision. The reason they drag on is that many people don't know how to end them gracefully. Actually, ending an interview isn't hard to do at all, not if you follow a few simple steps:

First of all, you always set a time limit at the beginning of the interview and always let the candidate know at the start when the interview must come to an end. In most cases, a half-hour should be sufficient. Second, you should give clues to the candidate that will suggest the interview is nearing its end. For instance, if you're using a pencil or pen, put it aside. If you wear glasses for reading only, take them off and put them away.

But whichever way you choose to end the interview, be sure to do it on the appropriate note—appropriate, that is, with respect to how good the candidate appears to you. If the candidate is somebody you definitely want, make sure the person knows you're actively interested. If the person is a "maybe," say that you're interested but that you want time to think it over. If the person is a definite "no," be polite but noncommital. "You have a fine record," you might say, "but I have other people to see. I'll let you know if we're interested." Whatever you do, don't say anything that might provoke a confrontation.

How to Handle References

It takes time and energy to follow through on a reference, but it is time and energy well spent—provided that you go about the process in the proper way. To begin with, you can all but ignore written references handed directly to you by the candidate. Such references are often written on the day of termination and could well reflect more guilt than accuracy. Second, see if you can get references from people who were not mentioned by the candidate; and while you're talking to a person listed as a reference, see if you can get still other names of people who know the candidate.

I would also recommend that you check your references by phone instead of by mail, because many people are reluctant to put derogatory remarks down on paper. Finally, if the position you're filling is important enough, it's not a bad idea to make a personal visit to the person giving the reference. People are usually more candid when you're face to face with them than they are over the phone or in a letter.

Getting the Person You Want

It is one thing to find somebody you'd like to hire but something else again to land that candidate, especially if the applicant is a coveted prospect. The better the candidates, the more likely they are to be in demand, so when you have an opportunity to hire good people, take action. Here are four guidelines:

1. *Don't delay the offer:* If a candidate is right for the job, don't hesitate to make an offer. You can always hire someone *contingent* upon his or her references checking out.
2. *Limit the number of decision makers:* The more people involved in the hiring decision, the longer it's going to take to hire and the greater the chances the person you eventually choose will be a compromise candidate.
3. *Set an early starting date:* The longer the time between the job offer and the starting date, the greater the risk of losing a good prospect. Losing a good prospect because of a delay happens more often than you might think. You think you've "hired" somebody, but before the person starts, another company comes along and makes a better offer.
4. *Don't fall into the "first one interviewed" trap:* Our studies show that the first person interviewed frequently doesn't get the job, even when that person may be the most qualified. Don't let this quirk cost you a good employee.

GETTING THE MOST OUT OF YOUR PEOPLE

Hiring the best people is one thing. Getting the most out of them is something else again. As any good manager knows, getting the most out of the people who work for you is almost a job unto itself and represents your most important managerial function. As I mentioned earlier, the very essence of managing is being able to handle people.

Robert Maynard, CPA, a partner and the national director of human resources for Price Waterhouse, attributes much of the success he's enjoyed to the fact that early in his career he was "well managed." "I remember a supervisor I had," he says, "who sat down with me one day and spelled out what I was doing right and what I was doing wrong. I can remember being upset, at first, about his criticisms, but once I stopped to think about it, I realized he was right, and I accepted the fact that I had to do something about my weaknesses. This was the first truly effective counseling I'd ever received, and it made a huge difference in my career."

Robert Maynard was fortunate. He had a manager who understood that there is more to managing than making sure that tasks are completed. He worked for a manager who cared enough about Maynard to criticize him constructively, a manager, in short, who understood that the key to managing is knowing how to get along with people. Let's look at some of the specific "people skills" that are basic to successful managing.

1. *Get to know your people:* To manage well, you need to know your staff members well. You need to be sensitive to their personality characteristics, their work patterns, and their career aspirations. You need to know—or to have a good idea of—which of your staff members are motivated primarily by financial gain and which of them are motivated by more intrinsic goals. You need to know how well each of them works under pressure and how sensitive each one is to criticism. More important, you need to be able to use this knowledge so that you can customize the way you handle each member of your staff.

   The best way to get this information is to be alert to it. You should be aware, for instance, of how each staff member interacts with the rest of the staff. You should also make it a point, as much you can, to meet one on one with staff members (assuming you're not supervising hundreds of people) so that you can find out directly from them what their feelings are about their jobs and how you might help them improve on the job. These talks can—and should be—informal, and should not exclude any staff members. Having these talks with only part of your staff will convey the impression of favoritism.

2. *Set tangible goals:* If you don't tell the people who work under you exactly what you expect from them, you're committing one of the cardinal sins of managing, and you'll pay for it in different ways. Those of your staff members who lack initiative will stagnate and produce very little. Those who are creative and energetic will set their goals on the basis of their own personal objectives. In both instances, the productivity in your department will suffer.

   There is more to setting tangible goals than meets the eye. For instance, the tendency among most managers is to assume that the staff member understands the goal and understands the rationale behind the goal. Both assumptions will get you into trouble, which is why I've always felt that when it comes to spelling out what you want, you can never be *too* specific. Far from resenting you for being so specific, most of your staff members will be grateful they're working for somebody who knows what he or she is looking for.

3. *Learn how to delegate:* Delegating doesn't come naturally. You have to learn how to do it, and the learning process, for some people, takes years. Accountants I've observed who have trouble delegating fall into one of two extremes: those who *over*delegate and those who *under*delegate. Overdelegators delegate tasks that go beyond the capability of their staff members. Underdelegators are simply afraid to let go of the reins.

The many discussions I've had with accountants about delegating have convinced me that probably the most crucial factor in delegating is confidence: in yourself and in your staff. If you lack confidence in yourself, you won't be able to accept the fact that you can't do everything yourself. You'll worry that in the event there is a mistake, you may not be able to survive it. If you lack confidence in your staff members, you won't delegate for fear that the job won't get done. There isn't much I can tell you if your reason for not delegating is a lack of confidence in yourself. If you lack confidence in your staff, it's clear that you haven't hired the right people, so your problem has less to do with delegating than it does with choosing the right staff.

An excellent exercise for accountants who want to improve their ability to delegate is to take a pad and list all the tasks that you now perform during a typical week. Once you've done this, examine each task and ask yourself if it's a task that only *you* can perform. If this is not the case, ask yourself why you are not delegating it.

I ought to stress, too, because it's so fundamental, that delegating involves far more than dropping a job in somebody's lap and expecting it to be done to your specifications. Depending on the nature of the work and the person to whom you're delegating it, you may have to spend some time explaining exactly what you want done, and you may have to nurse the person through the first phases of the job. Many accountants lack the patience to do this. As a result, they try for a while to delegate and then, when the results are not satisfactory, go back to trying to do everything themselves.

"A good manager," says Don Prince, from our Pittsburgh office, "doesn't just give orders but always explains the logic behind the orders." The intelligent manager, in other words, invests the time in order to be able to delegate *more* as the staff member becomes increasingly knowledgeable and competent.

One last observation about delegating. You need to be flexible. The ability of a staff member to assume responsibility will vary not only according to that staff member's level of skill or knowledge but also according to the task itself. You have to vary your strategy from job to job. In other words, when you delegate, you have to consider both the person and the assignment.

4. *Praise staff members for jobs well done:* Praise is the most inexpensive way to motivate staff members, so don't be stingy with it. Don't praise when it's not called for; on the other hand, if you don't let your staff members know when they've done a good job, you're failing in a crucial aspect of leadership.

Many accountants are uncomfortable giving praise, possibly because they themselves worked for superiors who were not particularly generous with their praise. Yet once you begin praising, it will become easier and easier. Eventually it will be almost second nature.

Some advice on giving praise:

- *Be as specific as possible:* Instead of saying, "Great job," add something specific about the project that was good. "I particularly liked the way you handled the overview section."
- *Don't do it grudgingly:* If you're going to praise somebody, make it count. You might want to call the person into the office to do it. Another nice touch is to send a small note, even if you see the person every day.
- *Be sincere:* Your staff members will be sensitive not only to the praise you give them, but also to the tone you use in giving the praise.
- *Let others know about it:* When a member of your staff passes the CPA examination, for example, let the rest of your staff know about it. If a staff member gets an article published, make sure the article gets circulated among your staff, clients, or customers—if appropriate.
- *Give tangible rewards:* Good work should be rewarded not only with praise but also with something the staff member will value. Obviously, you can't keep giving raises every time someone does a good job, but there are nonmonetary ways of rewarding a job well done. If it's consistent with company policy, you might give somebody a day off. And don't ignore the importance of appropriate titles, such as cost accounting specialist or retail audit manager. Some talented accountants leave public and management accounting for a position that gives them a more impressive title. I've found that staff personnel with suitable titles are likely to be more satisfied with their firms than those without titles.

5. *Criticize constructively:* The motivating power of the praise you give your staff members will be even stronger if you are also able, when

necessary, to give solid *constructive* criticism. To ignore it when one of your staff members is not performing well is to do both of you a disservice. Most surveys show strongly that employees welcome criticism, if they perceive that the criticism is fair and has the firm's and the employees' best interests at heart. When the time comes to criticize, be sure you do it in private. If at all possible, try to preface any criticism with a few words of praise.

DON'T AGONIZE
OVER DECISIONS

One of the skills that good managers are supposed to have is the ability to make good decisions. Yet, as industrial psychologist Stephen Temlock points out, "If you're managing well, you don't make all that many decisions. You're mainly monitoring the decisions of others."

The point bears repeating. I know of many accountants for whom decision making is the most agonizing part of their job, and, in many cases, the decisions are not decisions they should be concerned with in the first place. Says Temlock, "If you're making too many decisions yourself, it means you don't have the right people or you don't have confidence in those people."

As a manager, you can't ignore decision making, but it's worth pointing out that experienced managers worry far less about decision making than novice managers. "One of the skills that many executives never learn," says Irving S. Shapiro, the retired chairman of DuPont, "is when *not* to make a decision." Shapiro feels that managers will very often make a decision prematurely, without adequate facts. "What most people don't realize," he says, "is that every time you make a decision you run about a 50-50 risk of making the wrong decision. There isn't a business person around who doesn't look back at the end of each day and wonder how he survived."

One well-known accountant who developed an effective reputation for decision making was ITT's Harold Geneen. According to financial expert Felix Rohatyn, who worked for many years under Geneen and who was profiled in the January 24, 1983, issue of *The New Yorker,* Geneen had a cardinal rule about decision making. Said Rohatyn: "Geneen's rule was that if you wait to make an important decision until all the information that you might want is in, you will never make it in time. Depending on the risks, on what the stakes are, you have to settle for 75, 70, or 65 percent of the information that you need, and, on the basis of what you have, make your decision and go, because the time and the cost of getting, say, the last 25 percent are not commensurate with what you gain from deferring the decision."

The overall point here is not to let the decision-making aspect of your job overwhelm you. If you're having trouble making a decision, it's probably because of one or two reasons: one, you don't have all the facts; and two, you're too close to the situation to be objective. "What I do when I find myself having trouble with a decision," says William Morgan, "is to step away from it and let it sit for a while—if it's at all possible. Then I find that when I least expect it, when I'm driving or doing something else, I'll think about it and get an entirely different slant on the subject."

One final thought on decision making: You rarely have to make a major decision alone. Good managers, in fact, routinely seek input from staff members before making any major policy or operations change. In Japan, before managers make any decision, they are expected to gain a consensus from all the key people to be affected by the decision. This may be taking things too far, but decisions reached in this manner serve two important functions: One, they carry with them built-in acceptance. Two, they remove the burden of being right or wrong from the manager.

HOW TO TELL WHEN A STAFF MEMBER IS ABOUT TO QUIT

The last people you want on your staff are those who, for whatever reason, are looking elsewhere. The problem, though, is that most people looking for another job do their best to keep the news from their employers until they find something else. However, there are some signs that will give you an indication that somebody's planning to leave.

1. *Longer lunch hours:* Staff members who begin taking noticeably longer lunch hours could well be using the time for job interviews.
2. *Frequent absences:* Like longer lunch hours, a sudden increase in absences might indicate that the person is taking time off to go on job interviews.
3. *An increase in personal phone calls:* The calls may be coming from potential employers setting up interviews.
4. *Any change in communication attitude:* Take notice when a normally aggressive employee begins to act docile at staff meetings or a normally docile employee begins to act aggressive. It could mean that the employee no longer cares what management thinks.
5. *A change in vacation pattern:* Some employees who are planning an intensive job interview period will request an immediate vacation.
6. *A neater desk:* If the desk of an employee who usually has a sloppy desk suddenly appears neater than usual, it could mean that the employee is beginning to clear out personal belongings.

7. *A sudden improvement in grooming or appearance:* When staff members show up for work noticeably better dressed and groomed, they could be dressed that way because of possible job interviews.

WHAT TO DO ABOUT AN EMPLOYEE WHO PLANS TO LEAVE

If you have reason to think that a staff member is about to leave, your best policy is to act immediately. You should speak to this person and ask pointedly, "Are you looking to change jobs?" Most people won't lie to you when you confront them directly.

If the employee is somebody you want to stay, make an effort to reconcile differences. In some cases, a long talk in which you review the employee's future will bring problems to light and perhaps iron some of them out. On the other hand, if the person tells you, "I've just accepted a job," resist the temptation to make a counteroffer. Counteroffers, when accepted, will encourage other employees to use the same tactic. In addition, studies have shown that an employee who accepts a counteroffer rarely lasts more than a year.

WHEN FIRING BECOMES NECESSARY

Firing is something every good manager has to do now and then, and no manager ever gets accustomed to it. Probably the only consolation to the difficulty of firing someone is that surveys show most employees who get fired actually expect it, even though the day of reckoning may come as a shock.

Just as there is an art to hiring the right people, there is an art to terminating people. Here are a few principles to keep in mind:

1. *Do it in person:* If you hired the person who is to be fired, it's your responsibility to handle the firing and to do it in person. This is one responsibility you should never delegate.
2. *Don't drag it out:* Be tactful, but deliver the news early in the conversation. The longer you wait to give the bad news, the harder it is for the employee.
3. *Have all necessary information on hand:* The employee you let go has a right to know immediately whatever benefits are due. Have an adequate separation payment and the final check at the meeting.
4. *Be extra tactful:* Without lying, do your best to give the departing

employee an explanation that he or she can live with. The last thing
you want is a bitter ex-employee.

5. *Analyze what went wrong:* Our surveys indicate that most top executives place the blame on management when an employee is fired. You
have to ask yourself what led you to hire the person in the first place
and what you can do to prevent yourself from hiring the same type of
person again.

RATE YOURSELF AS A MANAGER

The following test should give you a general idea of how well you manage (assuming that you have a managerial position). If you're not a
manager as yet, you could take the test anyway and answer the questions
according to how you think you *might* perform as a manager. To take the
test, answer each question on a scale of 1 to 5, with 5 indicating that you
almost always do what the question asks and 1 indicating that you never
or hardly ever do it. When you've finished, you can rate yourself on a
scale of 1 to 100.

1. When you need to hire a new staff member, do you take the time
and make the effort necessary to hire the best possible person for
the job? _____

2. Do you take the time to orient new staff members so that they
understand not only their own jobs but also how their jobs fit into
the overall scheme of things? _____

3. Are you aware of the strengths and weaknesses of each of your staff
members? _____

4. Do you set the example you want your staff members to
follow? _____

5. Do you show a sincere interest in your staff members as *people,*
rather than simply as subordinates? _____

6. Are you aware of the career aspirations of each of your staff members? _____

7. Do you make it a point (if practicable) to meet one on one with
individual members of your staff? _____

8. Are you careful not to show favoritism to any member or members
of your staff? _____

9. Do all the members of your staff have clearly defined responsibilities
and the authority to carry out these responsibilities? _____

10. Do you have enough confidence in your staff members to trust their decisions on matters relating to their responsibilities? _____

11. When appropriate, do you involve your staff members in important decisions? _____

12. Do you try your best at staff meetings to encourage objective observations from members of your staff? _____

13. When you make assignments, are you sensitive to the workload? _____

14. Do you set *reasonable* deadlines when you make assignments? _____

15. Do you vary your supervisory style according to the personality of the staff member? _____

16. Do you make it a point to praise your staff members (when praise is justified) on a regular basis? _____

17. When you criticize staff members, do you try your best to be constructive? _____

18. Do you concern yourself with the advancement rate of your better staff members and do you help them as best you can to get ahead? _____

19. When a staff member quits, do you conduct an exit interview in order to determine the reasons for leaving? _____

20. Do you take time every now and then to evaluate your managerial effectiveness? _____

CHAPTER SEVEN **HOW TO MARKET YOURSELF**

Selling yourself is the most
important and most difficult
sale you can make.

It wasn't very long ago—as recently as 1978—that a chapter on marketing yourself would have been out of place in a book directed toward accountants. Prior to the 1978 change in the Code of Professional Conduct that removed the prohibition of advertising and public relations programs for CPAs, most accountants thought little about marketing. It was considered unethical, for instance, for public accountants actively to solicit clients who were being serviced by another accountant. And while it was okay to "develop a practice," it wasn't considered appropriate to take direct steps to promote your name: You had to be low-keyed and subtle.

Today, attitudes are changing. The idea that you never go directly to potential clients and ask them for business is, as far as many firms are concerned, a thing of the past. More and more firms are not only advertising their services but are also hiring professionals to handle their public relations.

Even given these changes in the profession as a whole, a great many accountants are still uncomfortable with the idea of marketing their companies and promoting themselves. A survey by the AICPA in 1981 revealed that two-thirds of its members still had negative attitudes toward uninvited solicitation and were still uncomfortable with the idea of seeking publicity, and there is no reason to think that management accountants are any less skittish about promoting themselves.

It's obvious, too, that most accountants do not do nearly enough to promote *themselves*. "A lot of accountants do a very adequate technical job," says Philip Chenok, "but do not get recognized. They are not known, they don't promote themselves in the company or outside the company. They don't write for the *Journal of Accountancy* or for state CPA society magazines or any professional publications. If they join a state CPA society, they don't show up at meetings and they don't attempt to get on committees. They go home, watch television, play with the kids, and go back to work the next day. I'm not saying you need to give up your social life, but I think to get ahead you need some visibility."

Why should accountants be this way? One possible reason is that many accountants simply don't know how to go about gaining visibility. A second reason may lie in the fact that many accountants are afraid of visibility. "With many accountants," says Isaac Assael, "it's a fear of putting themselves on the line. Some people are afraid that if they become well known, they'll become a target of criticism, and this may be why the general public has so little idea of what accountants do."

Whatever the reason that so many accountants aren't very good at marketing themselves, the fact remains that the ability to market yourself can have as much bearing on your career progress as anything else you do.

GAINING RECOGNITION

It is a safe assumption that the more people who are aware of who you are and what you can do, the more likely it is that your career will keep advancing. How do you go about gaining recognition while you're struggling each day simply to keep up with your responsibilities?

There is no one answer to the question, and a lot will depend on your specialty. Management accountants and accountants working for CPA firms, for instance, are not in a position to promote themselves as actively as accountants who work for themselves. But regardless of who you work for or what your specialty is, there are more ways than you might be aware of to gain recognition without devoting most of your time to the task and without violating any of the ethics of the accounting profession. Let's look at some of these ways.

GETTING INVOLVED IN ORGANIZATIONS

One of the easiest and most direct ways of gaining visibility is to become active in professional and community organizations. Indeed, if there is one thing in which nearly everyone at the top of the accounting profession believes, it's that the right kind of organizational involvement translates directly into career progress. Philip Chenok, for instance, recalls one managing partner of a medium-sized firm telling him about the time he devoted to the Institute (AICPA). Because he enjoyed the involvement so much, he ended up spending almost as much time working for the Institute as he did on his practice. "And the strange thing," says Chenok, "is that the more time this accountant devoted to the Institute, the more his practice grew and prospered."

There are any number of organizations in which the right kind of involvement can help your career. Joining professional associations, such as the American Institute of Certified Public Accountants, the National Association of Accountants, or your state CPA society, is essential, but it isn't enough to join. To get the most out of these affiliations, you need to be active in them. You have to join and become active on committees (particularly those committees that match your specialty).

"The more you get involved," says Marshall Fudge, a chartered accountant who owns our Toronto office, "the more recognition you get from peers." Fudge himself is the example that proves the point. More than simply getting involved in professional organizations, he helped on professional development committees, marked examinations, and wrote articles. These kinds of activities, he maintains, help you whether you go into public or private accounting.

Your group involvements need not be limited to accounting. Dan Kramer, as I mentioned before, attributes the large number of entertainment clients that he had during his public accounting career to the fact that he was always very interested in classical music. Other accountants have parlayed their interest in sports or civic organizations into more visibility and greater career success. Apart from these kinds of groups, you might want to consider organizations like the local chamber of commerce (especially if you have a private practice). If you're a management accountant you should belong to the trade associations that relate to your industry.

We've only scratched the surface. In every community there are civic organizations, executive groups, religious groups, educational groups, alumni associations, and country clubs. Clearly, you don't have the time to join all of them, so be selective. You're better off, I believe, being *active* and visible in a few organizations than being a name on countless membership rosters. To repeat, try to get active on those committees that deal with your field of interest. If you're a tax accountant, you should be on the tax committee and, ideally, should be heading it. Being the head says to the outside world that you're an expert. (Don't you tend to assume that the chief of surgery at a hospital is the best surgeon?)

Political parties, too, represent good opportunities for useful affiliations, albeit with some qualifications. Make sure, for one thing, that the job you do for the party relates in some way to your career interest. Also, don't allow your partisan politics to spill over into your office or, if you're a practicing CPA, to your clients. As long as you're careful about these things, most firms won't mind your getting involved in politics. Many, in fact, encourage these involvements.

All in all, then, the thing to remember about organizations is to choose those you become active in with care. Concentrate mainly on groups and affiliations in which you are likely to make the most contacts and your involvement will do the most to enhance your reputation.

GETTING INTO PRINT

Few things you do as an accountant will help your career more than getting articles published in trade and business journals. "If you can write well," notes Dr. Emanuel Saxe, "you have a built-in means of advertising yourself." Getting articles published makes you more of an authority. It looks good to your current company and it gets other firms interested in you. I can tell you from first-hand experience that personnel directors as well as recruiters follow articles in trade journals closely.

Writing articles can be especially difficult if, like most accountants, you've never done much writing. On the other hand, there is no great mystery to writing. I've never taken a writing course in my life, but I write well enough to get published. The reason is that I've worked hard on my writing. More important, I enjoy it and set aside time for it.

If you lack confidence in your ability to write, it may well be that you've never given it enough time. You might want to take a course or, at the very least, read a few books on writing. Remember, it's your expertise and your ideas that publications are looking for. As long as the article is reasonably well organized and the information is accurate and pertinent, the editors will do the final editing.

GETTING ARTICLES PUBLISHED

I've known accountants who, without being asked, have sent in finished articles to publications and had them published, but I don't recommend this strategy. Under most circumstances unsolicited articles do *not* get published (some magazines won't even accept them). In other words, you could be wasting a lot of effort.

The recommended procedure is to write a letter to the editor of the publication in which you briefly outline the kind of article you'd like to write. Professional writers call this a query letter, and here, from *How to Write Like a Pro*, by Barry Tarshis, are the guidelines to follow:

1. Be brief.
2. Make sure that the idea you suggest (*a*) is appropriate for the magazine you're writing to and (*b*) has not been covered by that magazine recently.
3. If you can make some personal connection early in the letter ("Jane Doe suggested I write you. . . ."), do so.
4. Be upbeat and positive, but don't oversell your idea. Avoid overstatements and don't hit the editor over the head with how much the article is needed. Let the editor decide.
5. Be as specific as you can in outlining the general content of the article.
6. Try to write naturally. When in doubt, write the same as you speak. Should you get the go-ahead to do the article, you'll be given a deadline, and I would urge you, particularly if this is your first article, to meet that deadline. If you're going to be late with the article, notify the publication well in advance. Apart from looking for accountants who know how to write, editors are anxious for accountants who can meet deadlines. The easier you make life for them, the more likely they'll be to invite you to write more articles.

WRITING LETTERS TO THE EDITOR

One of the simplest ways of getting your name known is to write letters to the editor. Don't waste your time writing about issues that don't relate to your specialty—not unless you can demonstrate something in the letter about your broad financial and business expertise. Regardless of how you might feel, say, about the dog-leash law or a new parking regulation in your town, a letter on these topics will not enhance your reputation as much as a letter that promotes the idea that you're an authority and a specialist. Also, the impression your letter leaves on the reader should be one that enhances your reputation as an authority.

There are some purely technical ground rules to follow when you're writing a letter to an editor. Your letter should be about the same length as other letters the publication prints. (Unless your name is Henry Kissinger, few newspapers or magazines will publish a letter that will fill most of the Letters to the Editor section.)

Another thing you have to be careful about when you write a letter to the editor is keeping the tone calm and factual. Apart from the fact that anger and emotion are difficult to convey effectively in a letter, editors usually worry about anything too incendiary. Finally, keep the focus of the letter as narrow as possible. Pick one topic, issue, or idea and try to stick to it throughout the letter.

The letter in Exhibit 2, which was published in the *Wall Street Journal,* illustrates the points I've just made. I wrote it in response to an article by Frank R. Beaudine. In his article, Beaudine made the point that some search consultants are troubled by candidates who insist that they be called only at home because "it conveys a feeling of insecurity."

I disagree. Far from showing insecurity, a person who has the recruiter call at home is prudent. Note that in the letter I get to the point immediately. Note, too, that even though I disagree with Beaudine's views, I do not attack him personally, and I'm careful about my tone. I also kept the letter brief. One other thing: I sent the letter by Federal Express, which means that the paper got it the next day, and it undoubtedly stood out on the editor's desk.

LETTERS TO THE EDITOR
Call Me at Home

Frank R. Beaudine, "Manager's Journal—What to Do When the Executive Recruiter Calls" (Dec. 27), writes: "Note of caution: Some search consultants are troubled by candidates who insist that they can be called only at home. It conveys the feeling of insecurity.

In my judgment candidates at all levels have to be concerned about jeopardizing their positions—particularly in these economic times. It is awkward, inappropriate and dangerous to conduct employment interviews on their employers' time. Candidates who request that recruiting calls be made to their homes are both sensible and prudent.

In addition, candidates who defer calls until after hours are showing respect for their current employers. People have every right to change jobs, but they should do it with maximum consideration for their employers and minimum risk to themselves.

ROBERT HALF
President
Robert Half International Inc.

EXHIBIT 2. Letter to the Editor. (Reprinted from *The Wall Street Journal,* December 30, 1982, with permission.)

PUBLIC SPEAKING

Like the ability to write well enough for publication, the ability to speak in front of groups can greatly enhance your image and increase your visibility. If the idea of speaking in front of a large group of people intimidates you, don't be too embarrassed. According to psychologist Philip Zimbardo, speaking in front of a crowd of strangers is probably one of the most widespread fears in the United States today.

Fortunately, there are plenty of opportunities for accountants who want to overcome their fear of speaking and improve their ability to speak in public, and I would urge you to take advantage of these programs. The only way you will overcome your reluctance to speak in front of groups is to do it a few times and recognize that if you know your material, there is nothing to fear.

An excellent way to gain more confidence as a public speaker is to begin speaking in front of groups that will give you the opportunity to gain experience but carry no risk to your reputation. For instance, the guidance counselor at your local high school would probably welcome the idea of your talking to a senior class about career opportunities in accounting. A local retiree club would undoubtedly be interested in what you might have to tell them about financial management. Once you've gained a little confidence, you can branch out to some of the local social, civic, and religious groups, all of whom look regularly for knowledgeable speakers.

To make things easy for yourself, you should develop two or three 20-minute to 30-minute speeches on general subjects that you can talk about in front of most groups. Here are some suggestions:

What to do when the IRS calls

Fringe programs for employees

How to manage household expenses

How to start your own business

Setting up your own accounting system

As far as preparing the speech goes, you have a couple of options. One is to hire a free-lance writer to write the speech for you. The other is to do it yourself, which isn't as difficult as you may think. Just make sure you keep your sentences short and your tone conversational. Remember, you're giving a speech, not a technical paper, and whatever you do, don't *read* the speech from a prepared text. Speak from brief notes. One page, 8½ × 11, should suffice for a half-hour talk.

Your opening is particularly important, but a good opening, contrary to what many people think, doesn't have to include a joke. In fact, unless you're an accomplished storyteller and are sure of a laugh, you shouldn't try to be funny at the start of a speech. If the joke doesn't work, it makes everybody feel ill at ease.

The best openings are anecdotes—provided, that is, that they relate to the theme of your speech. If you want to give the anecdote more credibility, make yourself a part of it. Barring the anecdote, try a quote.

PUBLICIZING THE SPEECH

Most of the time, if you are giving a speech to an organization, its public relations manager will send press releases to local papers. (You'll need an up-to-date—and good—photograph of yourself, as well as a brief written biography.) In the event that the group has no such person, you must take it upon yourself to write the release and to send it to the newspaper.

The release doesn't have to be elaborate. Here's how one might read:

> Local CPA to Speak
> at Friends of Library
> Meeting
> Linda Smith, a Certified Public Accountant with the firm of Jones and Smith, will be the featured speaker Monday evening, June 23, at the monthly Friends of Library meeting. Her topic will be *How to Start a Small Business.* Ms. Smith, a resident of Oakview for the past seven years, is a graduate of State College. She spent four years with the CPA firm of Brown and Brown before joining with Alvin Jones last year. She has lectured on the topic of starting a small business for several local groups, including the Chamber of Commerce.
> Anyone interested in attending the talk should contact the Library.

The release should be sent to the attention of the business-financial editor. Make sure you include a good black-and-white glossy of yourself, at least 5 × 7. You could write a similar release *after* you've given the speech, in which case you would include a paragraph or two that summarizes the points covered in the talk.

TEACHING A COURSE

Another good way for accountants to become better known in their communities is through teaching. Granted, there are some drawbacks. Teaching, particularly part-time, doesn't pay much. It takes time. (In addition to classroom lectures, there are lessons to prepare and papers to mark.) Also, teaching could add yet another burden to what is already a busy schedule.

On the other hand, teaching—as long as it doesn't interfere with everything else you're trying to do—can be rewarding in more ways than one. Teaching builds your credibility as an authority. Teaching forces you to keep current and thus imposes a discipline that might not be there if you were not teaching. It also encourages you to improve your communications skills and in this way helps your self-confidence. Once you learn how to keep the attention of a class for an hour or two, a half-hour speech in front of a large group is not difficult at all.

If you're going to teach, keep a couple of things in mind. First of all, I would never take on more than one course per semester (particularly if I had never taught before) and, if possible, I would only teach a course that met for one night a week. I would also be sure to teach a subject I knew backward and forward.

The best source for a teaching job, and the source with which you'll have the least trouble, is adult education classes through your high school. (They're a good place to gain experience.) Simply contact the school and let it know you're interested in teaching. Mention the subject you want to teach, the time you have available, and your credentials.

GETTING YOUR
NAME IN PRINT

Entertainment celebrities spend thousands of dollars a year on publicists whose chief job is to get the celebrities' names mentioned in a newspaper or on television. You can do it a lot less expensively. For example, do your best to get to know local business writers. The reason: When business writers are researching articles, they often need authoritative quotes. Almost invariably, they seek out the people they know.

There are several ways you might get to know your local business writers better. One way is to ask among your friends if anyone knows any of the business writers or editors and radio and TV personalities in your community and could introduce you to them. Another way is to attend special events—conferences, for instance—in which reporters are likely to be in attendance. Whenever you meet somebody connected with the media, introduce yourself and try to strike up a brief conversation. Follow up your discussion with a letter and perhaps an idea for an article.

Should a business writer eventually contact you to answer a question or make a comment, you should, of course, be as honest and forthright as possible. At the same time, be careful not to say anything that's going to get you in hot water with your firm or your clients. The best way to handle a sensitive question is to come right out and tell the reporter that you're not in a position to answer it. Unless you know the reporter very well—and even then you should be careful—don't give "off the record" comments. Most reporters will protect your identity, but you don't know what kind of pressure the reporter is under to come up with a quote or a comment.

RADIO AND TELEVISION APPEARANCES

If the notion of your appearing on a radio or television interview show seems outlandish to you, you could be selling yourself short. True, the possibilities of guest shots on shows like *Today* or *Good Morning America* are remote, but in your community there are any number of radio stations and, now with cable spreading throughout the country, any number of television stations in which someone who can talk intelligently about finance would be in demand.

Your chances of being asked to appear on these shows will be greater, of course, if you have built up any sort of reputation through articles or through public speaking. But even without this sort of reputation, there's nothing wrong with a brief letter to the producer of the show in which you describe how much you like the show and let your availability be known in the event that the show needs a financial specialist.

Should you be asked to appear on either a radio or a television program, enjoy the ego thrill for a few minutes and then get to work. Find out what sort of a show it is, who's doing the interviewing, and who else (if anybody) is going to be on a panel. In most cases, you'll be told ahead of time what the interviewer will ask you; even so, you should decide in advance the key points you want to convey.

If it's your first media appearance, you can expect to be nervous, but there are a number of things you can do to keep your nervousness under control. I recommend, for instance, that you practice answering questions in front of a mirror or into a tape recorder. I'm not talking about *memorizing* questions, but by answering aloud some of the questions you're likely to be asked, you can frequently isolate spots at which you might stumble during the actual interview.

During the interview itself, the best advice is to relax—which, of course, is no advice at all. What *will* help in the interview, however, is to watch the person (not the camera) asking you the question and to *listen* carefully to the question. The idea here is to get your mind to focus on the conversation and away from the fact that you're on television. It's not a panacea, but it might work for you.

CHAPTER EIGHT HOW TO MAKE THE RIGHT JOB MOVE

There are few things in life more important than your career.

I don't care how good an accountant you are, what your present position is, or how satisfied you may be in your current position. Based on turn-over statistics, there is a good chance that within a few years you're going to find yourself looking for another job. You're not likely to be fired, but maybe you'll become bored with your present job. Maybe your firm will be involved in a merger that will leave you with less responsibility and a less promising career horizon. Or maybe your firm will run into problems or bring in somebody above you with whom you can't get along.

I'm not trying to alarm you, but a basic principle of career planning is to be prepared for the unexpected. I've seen too many good accountants

95

who, when suddenly faced with the prospect of finding a new job (for whatever reason), have made critical mistakes. They've taken jobs they shouldn't have taken—jobs that not only diverted these accountants from their long-term career plans, but also often put them into dead-end situations. On the other hand, I've seen accountants whose careers have blossomed once they were forced to leave what they had thought was a secure position. In finding a new job, they also moved off in a career direction for which they were better suited.

In this chapter, we're going to focus on what you should—and shouldn't—be doing when you find yourself looking for a new job. The point I'm going to be stressing, above all, is that looking for a job is a job unto itself, and to be successful at this job—that is, to find the job that's right for you—you have to be as organized, as energetic, as diligent, and as hardworking as you would be in any job you've ever had.

WHEN TO THINK ABOUT LEAVING

There are two obvious reasons for leaving a job. The first is when you have no choice in the matter: You've been terminated or your firm seems to be doing its best to make life miserable for you. The second is when you've been offered a position that *clearly* is going to take you closer to your long-term career goal.

So much for the obvious situations. There are two less obvious times when it probably makes sense to leave a job: One is once you've begun to sense that your job is in jeopardy and prudence dictates that you jump before you're pushed. The other is when you've reached a decision that you've advanced about as far as you're going to advance in your present job and that if you don't make a move, your career will be stifled. Let's look at both situations.

HOW TO TELL WHEN YOUR JOB IS IN JEOPARDY

Except in the rarest of instances, you can sense ahead of time if your company may be preparing to let you go. Here are some of the key signs to look for:

1. *Consultants:* The sudden appearance of consultants often means that heads are going to roll. Often the consultants' findings reflect the preconceived opinions of management. If consultants are being

brought in, find out who in management is bringing them in, and try to analyze whether or not you're in their favor.

2. *Mergers:* Regardless of comments from old and new management that "no one will be replaced," mergers and acquisitions could mean trouble for you, depending on how the merger has been structured and how you're positioned in your company. In most cases, it's the people who work for the smaller firm and the firm that was acquired whose jobs are in the most jeopardy, particularly if there is a duplication of jobs.

3. *Silent treatment:* Even though they may not do it consciously, bosses who are about to fire someone will make it a point to avoid that person.

4. *Lack of special assignments:* Not getting special assignments you've been accustomed to getting is one of the most reliable signs that your job is in jeopardy. Accountants who are about to be fired are almost never asked to do special work prior to termination and obviously are not alerted to future assignments.

5. *No criticism:* When bosses who have made it a practice to criticize you suddenly stop the criticism, it may well mean that they've made up their minds that such criticism is a waste of time.

6. *Being left behind:* When those around you and beneath you are moving up and you're standing still, you can pretty much assume that you do not figure in your firm's long-range plans.

7. *Less responsibility:* When functions you've been handling routinely are transferred to someone else, don't be misled into thinking that the firm believes you've been working too hard. It may be a sign that they're thinking of replacing you but are waiting until they can locate and train the replacement.

8. *Business slump:* When business starts going bad, nobody's job is guaranteed. Your move, in the event business is bad and doesn't look as if it's going to get better, is to analyze how critical your job is to the operation. Be particularly concerned if you're a relative newcomer.

OTHER REASONS FOR LOOKING ELSEWHERE

Even when your job is *not* in jeopardy, there are still some situations in which your long-term career interests will be better served by looking elsewhere. Here are the key situations:

1. *You're dead-ended:* Most of the time, if you're honest with yourself, you can gauge your career prospects with your current firm. The simplest way to do this is to look at the positions above you, think

about the people who are holding these positions, and ask yourself if
someone with your background, credentials, and personal acceptabil-
ity would make a likely candidate.

2. *Your firm is not moving forward:* If your firm isn't getting ahead, you're
   not likely to get ahead either. The question, though, is why isn't the
   firm doing better? Is it progressive enough? Has top management lost
   its touch with the marketplace? Has the firm's specialty lost its luster?

Let me stress here that unless the situation in your current job is
intolerable, don't be too hasty about making a change. "If you're going
to make a change," cautions Harry Gilbert, "make sure it's for the right
reasons. Too often the job change is motivated by short-term impatience
rather than a result of long-term career planning." Gilbert warns, in
particular, about the "grass is always greener" syndrome in accounting.
"A lot of accountants know somebody who has maximized job changes
into major success stories," he says, "but what isn't recognized is the fact
that in most success stories, the key was timing. The job changes were
made only when the individuals were absolutely sure they could not do
better where they already were."

There is no need to belabor the point. You're the only person who can
determine whether your best interests will be served by staying in your
current position or by looking elsewhere. But Harry Gilbert's advice
seems to me to be well worth heeding. Says Gilbert: "If you're going to
make a move, do it on the basis of *your* timing and *your* career goals, and
not the fact that there may be just another job out there for you."

JOB HUNTING: SOME BASIC CONSIDERATIONS

In the event that you've decided (or it's been decided for you) to look for
a new job, the most important thing to bear in mind is that looking for a
job may be the hardest job you'll ever have. To be successful—to get the
kind of accounting job you truly want—you need to be energetic, persis-
tent, and opportunistic: You can't sit and wait for the job to find you.
You have to find the job and then engineer a campaign to capture it.
Above all, you must never forget that being qualified for a job is not
enough to guarantee you that job. It is not necessarily the most qualified
person who is hired; it is the person who is able to convince the person
doing the hiring that he or she is the best person for the job.

Your approach to finding a job should be well organized. Whether
you're working or not, you must still set aside a certain part of the week

for your job search campaign. Many accountants I know have the mistaken belief that looking for jobs is mainly a matter of answering a few ads, sending out a few letters, and then sitting back and waiting for job interviews to materialize.

It doesn't work like that. Job hunting involves an enormous amount of digging, calling, and planning. If you're not working, you could be spending as many as 25 hours a week on your job hunt and still not have enough time to do what should be done. If you're working, the very least you should be willing to spend on your job campaign is 10 hours a week.

What should you be doing all this time? You should be scanning want ads, writing letters, talking to other accountants, researching companies that might be interviewing you, and, probably most important, talking to people you know in order to find job leads. All of this is part of an organized job search routine. The tighter the system you devise to handle these tasks, the more successful your search is likely to be.

Apart from being well organized, there are a number of basic considerations about looking for a job that bear mention here. Some of them apply when you're out of work and looking. Others apply when you're still working. All of them are important.

1. *Keep up your appearance:* Looking for a job (whether you're working or not) can be a stressful situation and, if you're not careful, your appearance will suffer. As important as appearance is to your career success when you're working, it's doubly important when you're looking for work. Make sure whatever clothes you wear to interviews bring out the best in you. If necessary, buy *new* clothes. I know of some employment counselors who advise their clients to take a vacation before launching a job search. My advice is not to waste the time. Take the money you would have spent on a vacation and buy some clothes that will make you look good and feel good.

2. *Don't keep your job hunt a secret:* The only time you should ever keep your job search a secret is if you're still working. (In that case do everything in your power to keep your current company from finding out your intentions.) Keep in mind that of all the sources of job leads, none is more fruitful than your friends and business contacts. If *they're* not looking around for you, you're wasting one of your most valuable resources. Don't forget to contact former employers—if you left under good circumstances. They could manufacture a good job for you or recommend you to a colleague at another company.

3. *Be wary of blind ads:* If you're still working and looking for a job, I urge you to be very careful about so-called "blind" ads—ads that have a box number but don't reveal the company name. True, some ap-

pealing-looking jobs are often advertised in blind ads, but consider the risk. You have no idea who is getting your response. In the event the person who receives your letter knows your firm or your boss, you could find yourself without a job.

4. *Keep a lot of things going:* You're only looking for one job, but you improve the odds of getting a good job if you have extra irons in the fire. Whatever you do, don't make the mistake of assuming a particular job is in the bag before you've actually been hired.

PUTTING TOGETHER A WINNING RESUMÉ

The resumé is a necessary evil in any job-hunting situation. The reason I say "evil" is that nobody is going to hire you on the basis of your resumé alone, but your resumé could easily knock you out of the running, and for reasons that may have nothing to do with your qualifications.

The first principle about putting together a resumé is to resist the temptation to have it done by a professional. Our Burke survey shows that the great majority of CPA partners (72.5 percent), top corporate management (84 percent), and personnel directors (84 percent) said that they can detect when a resumé has been prepared professionally. Although most of those interviewed didn't feel that a professionally prepared resumé might hurt the chances of a candidate, a substantial minority took the opposite view. Some 10 percent of CPA partners who said they could detect a professionally prepared resumé also felt that it would hurt a candidate's chances, and about 20 percent of top management personnel and 18 percent of personnel directors and managers took the same position.

An even more important reason for doing the resumé yourself is that by doing so you are forced to examine precisely what you have to offer a prospective employer. Developing your own resumé compels you to examine your accomplishments and therefore to develop a perspective about yourself that invariably helps you to perform better in the job interview.

As you may know, there are different types of resumés. The most common is the chronological resumé, in which you list your experience from the present backward. Somewhat less common is the functional resumé, in which you organize the resumé according to specific categories of experience and not time. There is also a hybrid form, in which you combine elements of the two.

Generally speaking, you're better off with the chronological resumé.

The problem with the functional resumé is that some personnel directors feel that it has been written to conceal something—perhaps the fact that you've had too many jobs.

I'm not going to go into the details of how you write the resumé, but I would urge you to look at some of the books on getting jobs. There are a number of such books, including *The Robert Half Way to Get Hired in Today's Job Market,* and nearly all of them include ideas on resumés. However, a few points bear special mention:

1. *Keep it as brief as possible:* A resumé should never be more than two pages. The best way to keep it brief is to include only relevant information.

2. *Stress accomplishments:* Instead of just listing the positions you've held and the responsibilities that were part of those positions, make sure you list what you accomplished in those positions. If you were able to save your firm money through an idea or system you instituted, don't mention only the idea or system; communicate the fact that you saved money as well.

3. *Keep the tone businesslike:* Except for the final comment on your resumé (if you choose to include a comment), avoid the word "I" and keep the tone straightforward and direct throughout.

4. *Use active words:* Keep sentences brief and, if possible, start a sentence with an active verb: "Developed a system that produced detailed sales analysis."

5. *Don't mention race or religion:* You should also exclude membership in any organization that might indicate race or religion. These are not relevant. Experience and skill are.

6. *Be honest:* Under no circumstances should you write anything in the resumé that isn't truthful.

7. *Leave out the following:* Salary requirements (you can talk about them during the interview), references (you can supply them on request), photograph (no one expects it).

One more word about resumés. I have recommended to many accountants who were looking for jobs that they prepare not one but several different resumés, each truthful but emphasizing a somewhat different aspect of their experience. One of your resumés, for instance, might be for a public accounting position and another for management accounting. One resumé might be tailored to a position as a specialist, another to a position as a generalist. In certain situations, I would even recommend that you tailor a resumé to a specific company, assuming, that is, that you know of a specific job you want at that company.

WHOM TO SEEK OUT

There are several sources of job leads, the most obvious of which are want ads and personnel recruiters, and you should use all of them. However, the most fruitful source of job leads is the one that many accountants looking for a job fail to use to their best advantage: your own contacts. Simply put, a contact is anybody who, directly or indirectly, might produce a job lead for you. It could be a relative, a business associate, or a golf partner. The fact is that nearly everybody you know could be the source of a job lead.

Unfortunately, most accountants looking for a job fail to capitalize on their contacts. The reason, in many cases, is nothing more than pride—foolish pride, I might add. Embarrassed by their situation, uncomfortable about asking for "favors" or "imposing" on friends and acquaintances, many accountants make the most fundamental mistake they can make when they're looking for a job (and I mentioned this before): they keep it a secret.

Don't make the same mistake. In fact, the first thing you should do when you begin to organize your job search is to write down the names of *everybody* you know who even remotely might be able to give you a job lead. Then divide the list into two groups: those who might be in a position to help you *directly*—perhaps set up an interview for you—and those who might *know* people who could set up an interview for you. Remember, too, that the new people you meet on your search can become useful contacts, provided that you make a favorable impression. I can recall any number of occasions when accountants we sent out on job interviews didn't get the job we sent them out on, but so impressed the interviewer that they were given additional leads that eventually paid off.

I consider contacts so fundamental to job searching that I recommend to accountants looking for work that they collect as many names as they can in as many places as they can. Once you've started collecting the names, don't be shy about contacting them. As long as you're courteous and direct, the people you contact are not going to be angry with you for seeking their help.

PUBLICATIONS: BEYOND THE OBVIOUS

Naturally, if you're looking for work, you should be following the want ads of local papers, but there are some less obvious media sources for jobs that could yield even better results. For instance, if you're a public accountant, I strongly recommend that you subscribe to the *Public Accounting Report*. This monthly 16-page newsletter can give you a great deal of insight into what is going on in the profession and, in the process, provide some valuable job leads. By reading the section of the report that lists client moves from one CPA firm to another, you can get a good sense of where the jobs are in public accounting. Clearly a firm that is picking up new clients and losing very few is going to need personnel. You'll also get some insight into which branches of the large and medium-sized firms are getting the business.

Even if you're a management accountant, you might find the report useful. If you're looking for a controllership position—or its equivalent—you might look at a company switching CPA firms. Why? Because when a company changes CPA firms, there's a fairly good chance it may be in the process of changing its own financial personnel as well. A letter to the president or a high-level officer in which you outline your qualifications is a good idea as well.

Finally, you should pay close attention to the major business publications, such as *The Wall Street Journal, Forbes*, and *Business Week*. Look for signs of anything that could indicate an opportunity for you—a merger or acquisition, an unusually good year, a new CEO.

GETTING THE MOST
OUT OF A RECRUITER

My advice when it comes to selecting a personnel recruiter is to visit several of them and let your judgment and instinct decide which of them suits you best. You'll probably do best, however, with a service that specializes in accounting and financial positions.

When you're dealing with recruiters, remember that you are not required to confine your search to one service (although if you're currently employed, it's probably a good idea to limit your search to one or two firms at the most, just to protect yourself). Also, you should be wary of personnel consultants, who, for a fee that can range between $1000 and $10,000 (I heard of one that charged a client $25,000), will guide you with your resumé and job search. If you elect to go that route, make sure you check the firm's references and contact the Better Business Bureau to find out if there have been any significant complaints.

HANDLING THE
JOB INTERVIEW

The job interview, as you probably know, is the single most important aspect of a job-hunting campaign. No matter how organized you are or how diligent you are about tracking down job leads, if you don't sell yourself in the job interview, your chances of getting the job you want are remote.

The best way to approach a job interview is to think of it as a kind of stage audition—a performance. You've been given a chance to "read" for a part, and it's up to you to perform in a way that will convince the interviewer that you're the person to hire.

DOING YOUR HOMEWORK

One of the cardinal rules of successful interviewing is never to go into an interview without being totally prepared for it. Go into the interview knowing as much about the organization interviewing you as you can. If it's a public accounting firm, you should know how big the firm is and what kind of clients it has. If it's a corporation, you should know its products, its size, and, if possible, its recent earnings. It would help, too, to know something about the company's strengths and weaknesses.

You can get this information from a variety of sources. Business directories—*Moody's, Dun & Bradstreet's, Standard & Poor's*—will give the basic information on larger companies, and you might also be able to find references to articles about these companies in *Reader's Guide to Periodical Literature*. As far as smaller companies are concerned, you'll have to be more resourceful. Your bank may be willing to get a Dun & Bradstreet report on a company for you. It would give you interesting historical background along with financial information. Try to talk to people who may know of the company. Better still, try to find an accountant who has worked for the firm in which you're interested.

I would strongly recommend, too, that you do what you can to find something out about the person interviewing you. Here again, library sources such as *Who's Who* might help, but you'll probably have to get the information from the people who recommended you for the interview. What sort of information should you look for? The type of personality— whether the person interviewing is aggressive, for instance—would be good to know, but just as useful is information about the person's interests.

Getting this information isn't always easy. It may take some digging— but it is extremely helpful. One of our Burke surveys showed that 75 percent of interviewers feel that not being familiar with their company hurts your chances of getting hired.

PREPARING FOR THE QUESTIONS

No two job interviews are exactly the same, but you can count on certain questions being asked. You can be sure, for instance, that the interviewer is going to ask you to talk a little about yourself and to give the reasons you can handle the job. If you're still working, you'll be asked why you want to leave your present job. From most interviewers, you can expect a question about your long-range goals, and a favorite question these days is what your weaknesses are.

There is no pat way to answer these questions, although there are some guidelines to bear in mind:

- *Be honest:* I can't think of any good reasons that would justify lying in a job interview, and I can think of a lot of reasons you shouldn't. The most obvious is that if an interviewer even remotely suspects you're lying, your chances of getting hired are nil. What do you do if you're asked a question that might not show you off in the best light? Answer the question quickly and move on to some other, more positive aspect of yourself. For instance, the interviewer says to you, "But you have no experience in the publishing industry, do you?" Your answer might be, "That's true, but I've worked for clients in the music industry and I think that there are some similarities." (Assuming, that is, that you actually had music industry clients.)

- *Be a good listener:* Concentrate on what the interviewer is saying to you, and be responsive. Nod when you're in agreement. Smile when it's appropriate to smile. Stay actively involved in the conversation.

- *Be careful of your body language:* More interviewers than you might think will be judging you on how you sit (be relaxed but don't slouch) and on whether or not you look them in the eye when you speak to them.

- *Keep your cool:* On rare occasions, you might run into an interviewer who seems to be doing everything possible to get you angry. On the outside chance that the interviewer is simply testing your ability to deal with pressure, keep your cool at all costs.

- *Brush up on your accounting:* Brush up particularly on the technical aspects of your specialty. You can be sure that your technical background will be discussed during the interview, but tailor the complexity of your response to the background of the interviewer. If you're talking to someone in personnel, for instance, make sure you avoid technical jargon.

One of the best ways I know of to prepare for the questions you're likely to be asked in a job interview is to practice answering questions in front of a mirror. Here are five questions of the many you might work with:

- What are your long-term career goals?
- Why do you want to work for our firm?
- What can you offer this company?
- Where do you see yourself in 5 years?
- What courses did you like best and least in school?

Practice answering these questions into a tape recorder while you sit in front of a mirror. As you do so, try to notice if your answers appear thoughtful. Check for disturbing mannerisms or lack of enough eye contact—anything that could distract an interviewer.

WHAT TO AVOID

In one of the Burke surveys we conducted a few years ago, we asked personnel directors to identify the most common mistakes made by candidates. Here's a brief summary of the findings:

1. *Poor grooming and inappropriate dress:* Interviewers, as we've already established, place great importance on how you look. They want someone, above all, who looks businesslike and professional.
2. *Lack of enthusiasm:* You're better off being *too* enthusiastic than being withdrawn or indifferent.
3. *Failure to ask questions about the job:* Interviewers like to see you reflect a serious interest in the duties and responsibilities of the job.
4. *Asking direct questions about salaries and fringes too early in the interview:* Save these questions until the offer is made.
5. *Desperation:* Despair may gain you sympathy, but it won't get you hired. In fact, showing desperation is almost guaranteed to lose you the offer.
6. *Exaggerating skills or accomplishments:* Interviewers can usually tell when you're stretching the truth and will almost invariably consider it a strike against you.
7. *Not knowing enough about the company:* Interviewers like to see that you're interested in the company (as opposed to a job for the sake of a job).
8. *Not maintaining eye contact:* Many interviewers perceive (rightly or wrongly) that if you fail to look them in the eye, you're trying to hide something.

9. *Showing a lack of confidence:* Interviewers expect you to be a little nervous at an interview, but there is a difference between being a little nervous and showing a lack of confidence. All things being equal, interviewers would prefer to see you overconfident rather than underconfident.

SHOULD YOU TAKE THE OFFER?

Not getting an offer after a job interview can be depressing, but being offered—and taking—the wrong job can be much worse: Not only can it lock you into an unhappy situation, but it can also set your career plans back for years. "It can be a tough situation," says Kenneth S. Asch, our Long Island office franchisee. "A lot of accountants are very flattered when the first offer comes in—particularly if the money is good. But what they don't do is consider the job within the framework of an overall career plan."

Don't misunderstand me. Career planning is an academic point if you've been out of work for several months, but with most accountants the situation isn't that critical. Kenneth Asch told me of one young public accountant, for instance, who had been making $32,000 and wanted to move into private accounting. She had two offers: One was for an industrial company and paid $38,000. The other was to take over the branch office of a bank and paid $40,000. The accountant chose the bank job only because it paid more money, not realizing that the career potential in the other job was far greater.

Another mistake many accountants make when it comes to a job offer is to concern themselves too much with the job and not enough with the firm or company. There are exceptions, I grant you, but for the most part the better the firm you join, the better your career interests will be served. Notice that I didn't say "bigger," for size isn't the issue. Quality is. "All things considered," says Alex Cohen of *The Practical Accountant,* "you should look for a firm that's going to help you get ahead, a firm with a good reputation and expertise and management who are respected and knowledgeable. You want a firm of high quality standards that brings people along, that has a liberal partnership program and esprit de corps."

But how do you decide how good a firm is before you work for it? There are any number of barometers you can use, but here, to my mind, are hallmarks of quality firms in public accounting and in industry at large.

- They're in a growth pattern.
- They enjoy an excellent reputation among other firms.
- They do not have *excessive* turnover.
- They encourage employees to get involved with professional societies (to the point of paying the dues).
- They put part of their earnings back into the firm.
- They're headed by a management team rather than by one person.
- They have a reasonably rapid rate of advancement.

Let me point out that some of the firms that meet these criteria might not necessarily be right for you, depending on your career expectations and depending, too, on whether you're in public accounting or management accounting. In public accounting, for instance, you should never join a firm unless you fully understand—and support—the company's partnership philosophy and policy. The better firms will be honest with you when you question them about their partnership policy. You can get a general idea of how quickly they tend to promote to partner and what kind of financial obligations would accrue if you were to become a partner. You should also be able to get an idea of what qualities the firm is looking for in a partner.

It's difficult to set up any sort of evaluative scale on the various partnership policies in public accounting. In the end, it's a matter of which policy suits you best. The point to bear in mind here is that you should find out as much as you can about these policies and other policies before you join any firm. After all, you're making one of the biggest and most important decisions of your life. It's a decision that deserves all the time you can give it.

CONCLUSION

Success takes just a little more work than failure.

What I have tried to do in this book is to share with you some of what I have observed and learned over the past 35 years about career success in accounting and what some of today's most successful accountants and business people have to say about the subject. As you realize by now, neither I nor any of the people I interviewed for this book offered you any magic formulas to achieve career success, and we didn't offer any short cuts, either. As I mentioned at the start of Chapter Two, the only easy way to success is to work hard.

On the other hand, the amount of work embodied in most of the advice found throughout this book is not as much as you might think, not if you're truly dedicated to achieving career success and not if you begin to implement this advice in systematic fashion. How much extra time would it take you, for instance, to look as good as you're capable of looking each day when you go to work? How much harder would you have to work to establish yourself as one of the main contributors in your firm? And how deep an intrusion into your personal life would there be if you spent two or three nights a month to become active in a professional group, or if you were to give speeches to local groups once every six weeks or so or write two or three articles a year worthy of publication?

No, time isn't the obstacle. The obstacle is commitment: making up your mind that you *want* to get the most you can out of your career, that

109

you're worthy and deserving of this success, and, finally, that whatever small sacrifices you may have to make will more than pay for themselves in the long run. The mere fact that you're an accountant indicates that you already have the basic tools for success. How far these tools will take you is entirely up to you.

APPENDIX

On the following pages are highlights from the Accountant Attitude Study conducted by Burke Marketing Research for Robert Half International Inc. The purpose of the study was to determine attitudes among various executives, both in and out of accounting, with regard to the accounting profession.

Appendix Table A. Highlights from Burke Accountant Attitude Study

Survey statements	Responses, %, from			
	Chief financial officers	CPA partners	Top corporate management	Corporate personnel directors
Would choose accounting as profession again				
Agree strongly	66.7	68.6	28.0	
Agree somewhat	13.7	21.6	46.0	
Neither agree nor disagree	2.0	2.0	16.0	
Disagree somewhat	9.5	3.9	8.0	
Disagree strongly	5.9	3.9	—	
Don't know	2.0	—	2.0	
Opportunities in today's business climate better than ever for accountants				
Agree strongly	64.7	54.9	30.0	34.0
Agree somewhat	27.5	37.3	50.0	52.0
Neither agree nor disagree	5.9	3.9	8.0	6.0
Disagree somewhat	2.0	2.0	12.0	6.0
Disagree strongly	—	2.0	—	2.0
Accounting is an excellent field for *men* looking to advance quickly				
Agree strongly	35.3	37.3	16.0	10.0
Agree somewhat	35.3	49.0	42.8	34.0
Neither agree nor disagree	9.8	—	26.0	26.0
Disagree somewhat	15.7	11.8	12.0	16.0
Disagree strongly	2.0	2.0	2.0	12.0
Don't know	2.0	—	2.0	2.0
Accounting is an excellent field for *women* looking to advance quickly				
Agree strongly	62.7	47.1	34.0	26.0
Agree somewhat	29.4	33.3	50.0	36.0

Appendix Table A (*continued*). Highlights from Burke Accountant Attitude Study

Survey statements	Responses, %, from			
	Chief financial officers	CPA partners	Top corporate management	Corporate personnel directors
Accounting is an excellent field for *women* looking to advance quickly				
Neither agree nor disagree	2.0	7.8	10.0	16.0
Disagree somewhat	3.9	5.9	4.0	14.0
Disagree strongly	—	3.9	2.0	6.0
Don't know	2.0	2.0	—	2.0
Accountants are entrepreneurial in their thinking				
Agree strongly	5.9	25.5		
Agree somewhat	31.4	41.2		
Neither agree nor disagree	11.5	5.9		
Disagree somewhat	37.3	13.7		
Disagree strongly	11.8	5.9		
Don't know	2.0	7.8		
Public accountants lack education and training in economics				
Agree strongly	5.9	5.9		
Agree somewhat	31.4	17.6		
Neither agree nor disagree	9.8	11.8		
Disagree somewhat	43.1	39.2		
Disagree strongly	5.9	25.5		
Don't know	3.9	—		
Public accountants lack education and training in budgets				
Agree strongly	7.8	3.9		
Agree somewhat	35.3	23.5		
Neither agree nor disagree	3.9	7.8		
Disagree somewhat	35.3	41.2		
Disagree strongly	15.7	23.5		
Don't know	2.0	—		
Public accounts lack education and training in cost accounting				
Agree strongly	9.8	11.8		
Agree somewhat	29.4	23.5		
Neither agree nor disagree	5.9	7.8		
Disagree somewhat	35.3	31.4		
Disagree strongly	17.6	23.5		
Don't know	2.0	2.0		
Accountant with MBA more likely to get ahead than one without MBA				
Agree strongly	33.3	31.4	50.0	38.0
Agree somewhat	39.2	27.5	32.0	46.0
Neither agree nor disagree	9.8	13.7	6.0	4.0

Appendix Table A (*continued*). Highlights from Burke Accountant Attitude Study

Survey statements	Chief financial officers	CPA partners	Top corporate management	Corporate personnel directors
	Responses, %, from			

Accountant with MBA more likely to get ahead than one without MBA

Disagree somewhat	9.8	17.6	4.0	8.0
Disagree strongly	5.9	9.8	4.0	4.0
Don't know	2.0	—	4.0	—

Accountants undervalued/underpaid in public accounting

Agree strongly	—	21.6		
Agree somewhat	13.7	19.6		
Neither agree nor disagree	13.7	11.8		
Disagree somewhat	43.1	39.2		
Disagree strongly	21.6	7.8		
Don't know	7.8	—		

Accountants undervalued/underpaid in management accounting

Agree strongly	7.8	7.8	4.0	6.0
Agree somewhat	19.6	11.8	14.0	16.0
Neither agree nor disagree	21.6	23.5	26.0	8.0
Disagree somewhat	37.3	41.2	44.0	46.0
Disagree strongly	11.8	5.9	8.0	20.0
Don't know	2.0	9.8	4.0	4.0

Easier for articulate accountants to get ahead in public accounting

Agree strongly	72.5	78.4		
Agree somewhat	21.6	17.6		
Neither agree nor disagree	2.0	2.0		
Disagree somewhat	2.0	2.0		
Disagree strongly	—	—		
Don't know	2.0	—		

Easier for articulate accountants to get ahead in management accounting

Agree strongly	72.5	62.7	60.0	66.0
Agree somewhat	27.5	21.6	38.0	34.0
Neither agree nor disagree	—	9.8	—	—
Disagree somewhat	—	3.9	2.0	—
Disagree strongly	—	—	—	—
Don't know	—	2.0	—	—

Accountants in business for themselves are usually successful

Agree strongly	—	19.6	—	6.0
Agree somewhat	25.5	52.9	24.0	24.0
Neither agree nor disagree	31.4	13.7	44.0	40.0
Disagree somewhat	25.5	7.8	14.0	14.0

Appendix Table A (*continued*).   Highlights from Burke Accountant Attitude Study

Survey statements	Responses, %, from			
	Chief financial officers	CPA partners	Top corporate management	Corporate personnel directors
Accountants in business for themselves are usually successful				
Disagree strongly	2.0	—	4.0	2.0
Don't know	15.7	5.9	14.0	14.0
Importance of being a CPA in public accounting				
Very important	92.2	98.0		
Somewhat important	5.9	2.0		
Neither important nor unimportant	—	—		
Somewhat unimportant	—	—		
Very unimportant	—	—		
Don't know	2.0	—		
Importance of being a CPA in management accounting				
Very important	11.8	29.4	32.0	30.0
Somewhat important	62.7	58.8	56.0	50.0
Neither important nor unimportant	11.8	—	2.0	4.0
Somewhat unimportant	9.8	5.9	8.0	12.0
Very unimportant	3.9	—	—	4.0
Don't know	—	5.9	2.0	—
Importance of having knowledge of computers in public accounting				
Very important	62.7	45.1		
Somewhat important	33.3	52.9		
Neither important nor unimportant	3.9	2.0		
Somewhat unimportant	—	—		
Very unimportant	—	—		
Don't know	—	—		
Importance of having knowledge of computers in management accounting				
Very important	66.7	72.5	70.0	74.0
Somewhat important	33.3	21.6	24.0	24.0
Neither important nor unimportant	—	2.0	6.0	—
Somewhat unimportant	—	2.0	—	2.0
Very unimportant	—	—	—	—
Don't know	—	2.0	—	—
Importance of specializing within public accounting				
Very important	23.5	33.3		
Somewhat important	41.2	35.3		

Appendix Table A (*continued*). Highlights from Burke Accountant Attitude Study

Survey statements	Chief financial officers	CPA partners	Top corporate management	Corporate personnel directors
		Responses, %, from		

Importance of specializing within public accounting

Neither important nor unimportant	9.8	13.7		
Somewhat unimportant	11.8	15.7		
Very unimportant	2.0	2.0		
Don't know	11.8	—		

Importance of specializing within management accounting

Very important	2.0	13.7		
Somewhat important	31.4	33.3		
Neither important nor unimportant	11.8	19.6		
Somewhat unimportant	33.3	23.5		
Very unimportant	15.7	3.9		
Don't know	5.9	5.9		

Importance of belonging to a trade association

Very important	2.0	13.7		
Somewhat important	43.1	43.1		
Neither important nor unimportant	13.7	9.8		
Somewhat unimportant	25.5	25.5		
Very unimportant	11.8	5.9		
Don't know	3.9	2.0		

Importance of having articles published

Very important	2.0	3.9		
Somewhat important	21.6	33.3		
Neither important nor unimportant	25.5	11.8		
Somewhat unimportant	29.4	35.3		
Very unimportant	19.6	15.7		
Don't know	2.0	—		

Importance of assisting in public service

Very important	5.9	25.5		
Somewhat important	45.1	47.1		
Neither important nor unimportant	19.6	11.8		
Somewhat unimportant	21.6	9.8		
Very unimportant	5.9	3.9		
Don't know	2.0	2.0		

Appendix Table A (*continued*).   Highlights from Burke Accountant Attitude Study

Survey statements	Responses, %, from			
	Chief financial officers	CPA partners	Top corporate management	Corporate personnel directors
Importance of CMA				
Very important	2.0	2.0		
Somewhat important	31.4	31.4		
Neither important nor unimportant	15.7	7.8		
Somewhat unimportant	25.5	5.9		
Very unimportant	9.8	2.0		
Don't know	—	7.8		
Not aware of CMA	15.7	43.1	62.0	58.0
Public accountants have ability to get along well with people				
Agree strongly	15.7	41.2	10.0	14.0
Agree somewhat	54.9	43.1	46.0	46.0
Neither agree nor disagree	19.6	5.9	26.0	25.0
Disagree somewhat	5.9	5.9	16.0	6.0
Disagree strongly	—	—	—	2.0
Don't know	3.9	3.9	2.0	4.0
Public accountants have good communication skills				
Agree strongly	17.6	45.1	6.0	14.0
Agree somewhat	54.9	39.2	46.0	50.0
Neither agree nor disagree	17.6	5.9	22.0	18.0
Disagree somewhat	9.8	5.9	26.0	10.0
Disagree strongly	—	2.0	—	2.0
Don't know	—	2.0	—	6.0
Public accountants have a high level of technical skills				
Agree strongly	49.0	37.3	24.0	30.0
Agree somewhat	45.1	51.0	34.0	48.0
Neither agree nor disagree	5.9	2.0	22.0	14.0
Disagree somewhat	—	7.8	16.0	6.0
Disagree strongly	—	—	—	—
Don't know	—	2.0	4.0	2.0
Public accountants are highly intelligent				
Agree strongly	23.5	27.5	8.0	8.0
Agree somewhat	49.0	54.9	42.0	48.0
Neither agree nor disagree	19.5	13.7	36.0	30.0
Disagree somewhat	2.0	2.0	8.0	8.0
Disagree strongly	—	—	2.0	—
Don't know	5.9	2.0	4.0	6.0

Appendix Table A (*continued*). Highlights from Burke Accountant Attitude Study

Survey statements	Responses, %, from			
	Chief financial officers	CPA partners	Top corporate management	Corporate personnel directors
Public accountants are well-rounded business persons				
Agree strongly	—	21.6	—	6.0
Agree somewhat	37.3	35.3	26.0	32.0
Neither agree nor disagree	15.7	17.6	28.0	16.0
Disagree somewhat	37.3	23.5	38.0	34.0
Disagree strongly	5.9	—	4.0	8.0
Don't know	3.9	2.0	4.0	4.0
Management accountants are able to get along well with people				
Agree strongly	9.8	7.8	6.0	10.0
Agree somewhat	62.7	56.9	46.0	56.0
Neither agree nor disagree	21.6	17.6	30.0	22.0
Disagree somewhat	5.9	11.8	14.0	12.0
Disagree strongly	—	2.0	2.0	—
Don't know	—	3.9	2.0	—
Management accountants have good communication skills				
Agree strongly	15.7	19.6	8.0	12.0
Agree somewhat	39.2	47.1	42.0	54.0
Neither agree nor disagree	29.4	15.7	18.0	20.0
Disagree somewhat	13.7	13.7	30.0	14.0
Disagree strongly	—	2.0	—	—
Don't know	2.0	2.0	2.0	—
Management accountants have a high level of technical skills				
Agree strongly	15.7	13.7	14.0	18.0
Agree somewhat	68.6	58.8	48.0	60.0
Neither agree nor disagree	9.8	11.8	24.0	12.0
Disagree somewhat	3.9	11.8	12.0	10.0
Disagree strongly	—	—	—	—
Don't know	2.0	3.9	2.0	—
Management accountants are highly intelligent				
Agree strongly	11.8	13.7	8.0	8.0
Agree somewhat	58.8	62.7	42.0	58.0
Neither agree nor disagree	25.5	13.7	36.0	30.0
Disagree somewhat	2.0	5.9	10.0	2.0
Disagree strongly	—	—	2.0	—
Don't know	2.0	3.9	2.0	2.0

Appendix Table A (*continued*). Highlights from Burke Accountant Attitude Study

Survey statements	Chief financial officers	CPA partners	Top corporate management	Corporate personnel directors
	Responses, %, from			
Management accountants are well-rounded business persons				
Agree strongly	7.8	7.8	—	6.0
Agree somewhat	41.2	41.2	38.0	52.0
Neither agree nor disagree	27.5	15.7	24.0	14.0
Disagree somewhat	15.7	29.4	30.0	24.0
Disagree strongly	2.0	2.0	4.0	4.0
Don't know	5.9	3.9	4.0	—
Chief executive officer has strong accounting or finance background				
Yes	33.3	—	38.0	30.0
No	66.7	—	60.0	68.0
Don't know	—	—	2.0	2.0
Accountants are too numbers oriented				
Agree strongly		13.7	18.0	
Agree somewhat		54.9	52.0	
Neither agree nor disagree		7.8	8.0	
Disagree somewhat		13.7	18.0	
Disagree strongly		3.9	4.0	
Don't know		5.9	—	
Accountants lack imagination				
Agree strongly		3.9	14.0	
Agree somewhat		23.5	42.0	
Neither agree nor disagree		9.8	12.0	
Disagree somewhat		41.2	30.0	
Disagree strongly		17.6	2.0	
Don't know		3.9	—	
Accountants are poor listeners				
Agree strongly		2.0	2.0	
Agree somewhat		17.6	16.0	
Neither agree nor disagree		—	30.0	
Disagree somewhat		45.1	42.0	
Disagree strongly		33.3	8.0	
Don't know		2.0	2.0	
Accountants are poor communicators				
Agree strongly		2.0	4.0	
Agree somewhat		19.6	38.0	
Neither agree nor disagree		3.9	22.0	
Disagree somewhat		43.1	30.0	

Appendix Table A (*continued*). Highlights from Burke Accountant Attitude Study

	Responses, %, from			
Survey statements	Chief financial officers	CPA partners	Top corporate management	Corporate personnel directors
Accountants are poor communicators				
Disagree strongly		29.4	6.0	
Don't know		2.0	—	
Accountants are too conservative				
Agree strongly		7.8	8.0	
Agree somewhat		49.0	46.0	
Neither agree nor disagree		13.7	30.0	
Disagree somewhat		25.5	14.0	
Disagree strongly		2.0	2.0	
Don't know		2.0	—	
Accountants are not good decision makers				
Agree strongly		—	8.0	
Agree somewhat		13.7	24.0	
Neither agree nor disagree		3.9	28.0	
Disagree somewhat		52.9	40.0	
Disagree strongly		27.5	—	
Don't know		2.0	—	
Accountants are weak in managerial skills				
Agree strongly		3.9	6.0	
Agree somewhat		33.3	44.0	
Neither agree nor disagree		9.8	22.0	
Disagree somewhat		39.2	24.0	
Disagree strongly		11.8	2.0	
Don't know		2.0	2.0	

Appendix Table B. Queries from Burke Accountant Attitude Study

	Responses, %, from	
Survey questions	Chief financial officers	CPA partners
What single piece of advice would you give to accountants just starting out in public accounting? [a]		
Career path		
Get as much experience or as varied experience as possible	13.7	21.6

Appendix Table B (*continued*). Queries from Burke Accountant Attitude Study

Survey questions	Responses, %, from	
	Chief financial officers	CPA partners

What single piece of advice would you give to accountants just starting out in public accounting?[a]

Go with a big, a national, an established, or a growing firm	9.8	15.7
Do not specialize	5.9	5.9
Join a medium-sized, local firm	—	5.9
Specialize	—	3.9
Miscellaneous career path	9.8	5.9

Education and communication skills

Learn and get as much education as possible	9.8	23.5
Pass the examination for the CPA examination and get your certificate	11.8	7.8
Improve communication skills	5.9	3.9
Miscellaneous education and communication skills	2.0	—

Personal attitudes

Work hard and long hours	15.7	15.7
Persist. Stay with it for at least 5 years	5.9	9.8
Use common sense	5.9	2.0
Be patient and go slow	—	5.9
Miscellaneous personal attitudes	7.8	—

Miscellaneous

Explore other fields	5.9	2.0
Other miscellaneous	—	2.0
Don't know or none	11.8	3.9

What single piece of advice would you give to accountants just starting out in management accounting?[a]

Education and communication skills

Learn all you can about the business, company, or firm	25.5	7.8
Get CPA certificate	3.9	7.8
Get as much education as possible	3.9	5.9
Develop communication skills	7.8	2.0
Pass CMA examination or join CMA programs	3.9	2.0
Get a master's degree	3.9	2.0
Get into a management training program	2.0	2.0
Learn about data processing, systems, computer field	3.9	—
Stay abreast of current developments in the profession	2.0	—
Get the management certificate	2.0	—
Miscellaneous education and communication skills	5.9	2.0

Appendix Table B (*continued*). Queries from Burke Accountant Attitude Study

	Responses, %, from	
Survey questions	Chief financial officers	CPA partners

What single piece of advice would you give to accountants just starting out in management accounting?[a]

Personal attitudes		
Work hard, long hours, be conscientious	17.6	3.9
Get involved, be aggressive, visible, open	7.3	2.0
Be creative and innovative	2.0	3.9
Use common sense	2.0	2.0
Miscellaneous personal attitudes	2.0	5.9
Career path		
Get into public accounting first	2.0	11.8
Get as much experience and as varied experience as possible	7.8	2.0
Miscellaneous career path	7.8	3.9
Miscellaneous		
Other miscellaneous	—	5.9
Don't know or none	3.9	37.3

What single piece of advice would you give to accountants who are thinking of going into business for themselves?[a]

Career paths		
Get as much experience and as varied experience as possible	13.7	7.8
Have a good client base and develop clientele	7.8	7.8
Work for a large firm first	3.9	7.8
Be responsive to clients' needs and give them individual attention	3.9	5.9
Be well organized; keep good records, accounts, tax systems	2.0	3.9
Get a good partner	2.0	2.0
Set goals for yourself	2.0	2.0
Miscellaneous career paths	3.9	2.0
Personal attitudes		
Be prepared to work hard and keep long hours	7.8	11.8
Be patient and stick with it	—	5.9
Meet people and get involved in community activities	2.0	3.9
Miscellaneous personal attitudes	5.9	2.0
Education and communication skills		
Develop technical competence	2.0	7.8
Develop good communication skills	3.9	—
Specialize	2.0	2.0

Appendix Table B (*continued*). Queries from Burke Accountant Attitude Study

	Responses, %, from	
Survey questions	Chief financial officers	CPA partners

What single piece of advice would you give to accountants who are thinking of going into business for themselves? [a]

Education and communication skills		
Do a lot of research; know the field	—	3.9
Certification is important	2.0	2.0
Miscellaneous education	2.0	—
Miscellaneous		
Have enough working capitol	21.6	11.8
I wouldn't recommend it	9.8	7.8
Weigh the advantages and dis-advantages	3.9	—
Do it; the rewards are gratifying	—	3.9
Other miscellaneous	—	2.0
Don't know	21.6	15.7

What single piece of advice would you give management accountants who are thinking of going into public accounting? [a]

Career paths		
Work for a firm; work for a large firm	3.9	7.8
Do it early in your career	5.9	3.9
Specialize	3.9	2.0
It's better to go from public to management accounting	5.9	—
Develop business contacts	—	2.0
Get as much experience as possible	—	2.0
Miscellaneous career paths	5.9	13.7
Education		
Get a CPA certificate	13.7	9.8
Further education, review, brushup	7.8	11.8
Miscellaneous education	2.0	—
Personal attitudes		
Be prepared to work hard and keep long hours	7.8	11.8
You have to be flexible and adaptable to pressure and changes	2.0	9.8
Personal relationships are more important in public accounting	7.8	—
Stick with it; it takes a long time	2.0	2.0
Get active in civic activities	2.0	—
Miscellaneous personal attitudes	3.9	2.0

Appendix Table B (*continued*). Queries from Burke Accountant Attitude Study

	Responses, %, from	
Survey questions	Chief financial officers	CPA partners

What single piece of advice would you give management accountants who are thinking of going into public accounting?[a]

Miscellaneous		
They are totally different	3.9	13.7
Don't do it	9.8	3.9
Limited earnings in the beginning	3.9	3.9
Can make more money in management accounting	2.0	—
Other miscellaneous	5.9	—
Don't know or none	17.6	23.5

What single piece of advice would you give public accountants who are thinking of going into management accounting?[a]

Career path		
Know the type of business; learn about all aspects of the organization	17.6	3.9
Look for the opportunity for advancement	9.8	7.8
Know the firm's financial stability and prospects for future growth	5.9	5.9
Do some research; be sure of the field before going into it	—	7.8
Do not specialize; test different fields	3.9	—
Enter at a high level	2.0	—
Specialize	—	2.0
Miscellaneous career paths	7.8	—
Education and communication skills		
Learn to communicate with management and associates	5.9	3.9
Brush up on cost systems and cost accounting skills	3.9	2.0
Get CMA; enroll in a CMA program	3.9	—
Be fully qualified	3.9	—
Pursue an MBA	—	2.0
Understand computer analysis	—	2.0
Personal attitudes		
Use initiative and capabilities; demonstrate your skills	5.9	3.9
Work and study hard	2.0	2.0
Don't be too forceful	2.0	—
Miscellaneous personal attitudes	5.9	3.9
Miscellaneous		
Don't go into management; too routine; repetitious; less freedom	2.0	9.8

Appendix Table B (*continued*).   Queries from Burke Accountant Attitude Study

	Responses, %, from	
Survey questions	Chief financial officers	CPA partners

What single piece of advice would you give public accountants who are thinking of going into management accounting?[a]

Miscellaneous		
Do it; it's a good move	5.9	3.9
Be prepared to accept lower salary	2.0	—
Performance requirements are not as strict in public accounting	2.0	—
Other miscellaneous	5.9	2.0
Don't know	11.8	43.1

[a]Percentages do not add up to 100 percent because some respondents gave more than one answer.

Index

ABOUT THE AUTHOR

Robert Half is the president and founder of Robert Half International Inc., the world's largest recruiting organization for accountants, financial executives, and data processing personnel. Founded in 1948, this company pioneered the concept of specialized personnel services. Mr. Half is a graduate of New York University and a member of the American Institute of Certified Public Accountants, the New York State Society of Certified Public Accountants, the American Accounting Association, the National Association of Accountants, and the American Management Association. He is a past president of the Association of Personnel Consultants of New York. An internationally recognized authority in his field, Mr. Half has appeared as an expert witness before the U.S. Senate Subcommittee on Reports, Accounting, and Management; his views and expert commentary have been reported in most U.S. newspapers—including *The Wall Street Journal*—and in magazines such as *U.S. News and World Report, Business Week, Newsweek, Time, Fortune,* and *Forbes.* In addition, he has been heard on hundreds of radio programs and has been seen on national television in *Good Morning America* and the *Today Show.* He is also the author of the national best seller *The Robert Half Way to Get Hired in Today's Job Market.*